M000170389

In my fifty-three years of ministry, I have read many books on prayer—most of which came across as commanding or condemning. But Pastor Hank Kunneman has written about prayer in such a way that it activates a desire and appreciation for it. The truth Pastor Hank presents comes from a life of prayer and intimate relationship with Jesus Christ. This book should be read by every saint and minister who wants more of God's presence and desires to demonstrate Christ's power.

—Dr. Bill Hamon
Bishop of Christian International Ministries Network (CIMN)
Author of *Day of the Saints* and many other major books

As an apostle of God, I am privileged to meet people from all over the world, and most especially those who are apostles, teachers, evangelists, and prophets. I have never met anyone, however, who ministers and delivers the prophetic Word of the Lord to thousands of people with such preciseness as my friend Hank Kunneman. *Don't Leave God Alone* is a powerful book that teaches how to seek God's face until we see things change. This book will radically transform your life and bring the kingdom of God into your family, city, and nation.

—Guillermo Maldonado
Senior Pastor, El Rey Jesús Ministries
Miami, Florida

Because of the effect that Pastor Hank's ministry has had on my family and myself, I know that the fruit of his labor will bless the life of anyone who comes in contact with it. As you read this book, I encourage you to tap into and draw from the prophetic mantle on the words written in it. As deep as the revelation in this book is, the content is released in simplicity. It is attention grabbing, full of humor, easy to read, and moves the heart of God. And anything that moves the heart of God will change the hearts of men.

—Kimberly Daniels
Apostle and Overseer of Kimberly Daniels Ministries International
Jacksonville, Florida

Hank Kunneman has written a book that will encourage believers to pray with the confidence that one person can move God to intervene on the earth. Your prayers can affect the present generation and generations to come. Allow the revelation in this book to break any limitations and launch your prayer life into a new level of effectiveness and breakthrough. Hank's passion to see a group of powerful intercessors come forth is found in the words of this book. Receive an impartation as you read, and allow it to activate you to pray with more power and faith. Let miracles be released that will change the course of history and see the kingdom advance in the days to come.

—John Eckhardt
Apostle and Overseer of Crusaders Ministries
Chicago, Illinois

DON'T LEAVE GOD ALONE

HANK KUNNEMAN

Charisma
HOUSE
A STRANG COMPANY

Most Strang Communications/Charisma House/Siloam/FrontLine/Excel Books/Realms products are available at special quantity discounts for bulk purchase for sales promotions, premiums, fund-raising, and educational needs. For details, write Strang Communications/Charisma House/Siloam/FrontLine/Excel Books/Realms, 600 Rinehart Road, Lake Mary, Florida 32746, or telephone (407) 333-0600.

Don't Leave God Alone by Hank Kunneman
Published by Charisma House
A Strang Company
600 Rinehart Road
Lake Mary, Florida 32746
www.charismahouse.com

This book or parts thereof may not be reproduced in any form, stored in a retrieval system, or transmitted in any form by any means—electronic, mechanical, photocopy, recording, or otherwise—without prior written permission of the publisher, except as provided by United States of America copyright law.

Unless otherwise noted, all Scripture quotations are from the King James Version of the Bible.

Scripture quotations marked AMP are from the Amplified Bible. Old Testament copyright © 1965, 1987 by the Zondervan Corporation. The Amplified New Testament copyright © 1954, 1958, 1987 by the Lockman Foundation. Used by permission.

Scripture quotations marked CEV are from the Contemporary English Version, copyright © 1995 by the American Bible Society. Used by permission.

Scripture quotations marked NAS are from the New American Standard Bible. Copyright © 1960, 1962, 1963, 1968, 1971, 1972, 1973, 1975, 1977 by the Lockman Foundation. Used by permission. (www.Lockman.org)

Scripture quotations marked NIV are from the Holy Bible, New International Version. Copyright © 1973, 1978, 1984, International Bible Society. Used by permission.

Scripture quotations marked NKJV are from the New King James Version of the Bible. Copyright © 1979, 1980, 1982 by Thomas Nelson, Inc., publishers. Used by permission.

Scripture quotations marked NLT are from the Holy Bible, New Living Translation, copyright © 1996, 2004. Used by permission of Tyndale House Publishers, Inc., Wheaton, IL 60189. All rights reserved.

Scripture quotations marked THE MESSAGE are from The Message: The Bible in Contemporary English, copyright © 1993, 1994, 1995, 1996, 2000, 2001, 2002. Used by permission of NavPress Publishing Group.

Cover Design: John Hamilton Design (www.johnhamiltondesign.com)
Executive Design Director: Bill Johnson

Copyright © 2008 by Hank Kunneman
All rights reserved

Library of Congress Cataloging-in-Publication Data

Kunneman, Harry, 1948-
  Don't leave God alone / Hank Kunneman. -- 1st ed.
      p. cm.
   ISBN 978-1-59979-195-1
   1. Spiritual life--Christianity. I. Title.
   BV4501.3.K86 2008
   248.4--dc22

                                          2007045828

First Edition

08 09 10 11 12 — 987654321
Printed in the United States of America

ACKNOWLEDGMENTS

To my wife, Brenda,
and sons Matthew and Jonathan
for their love and encouragement.

Also to our office staff
and everyone at Lord of Hosts Church
for their prayers and support.

The greatest thanks of all to
my Lord and Savior Jesus Christ
for His great grace!

CONTENTS

FOREWORD

D ON'T LEAVE GOD ALONE is an amazing book—one that will
dramatically revolutionize your relationship with God! Within
its pages, Hank Kunneman, whom I respect both as a friend
and Christian leader, has grasped the heart cry of God. I appreciate
Hank very much, have been in his church, and have experienced the
Spirit of God in a most unusual way.

In this book you'll discover how dramatically your life will change
when you press into God like never before. Hank examines the lives of
some of the great men and women of faith who refused to leave God
alone and how they were blessed as a result. Their cries changed history,
their own lives, and the lives of thousands. In this book you'll learn
the key to getting God's attention and, yes, even changing God's mind
about situations in your life. The tenacity of Elijah, Elisha, Jacob, Moses,
King Hezekiah, the Syrophoenician woman, the woman with the issue
of blood, blind Bartimaeus, and the church in Acts will stir your faith
like never before. After reading their exploits, you too will become a
person who pursues God until His blessings overtake you!

I believe with my whole heart that if you have ever struggled to
receive a much-needed answer from God, if you are discouraged because
you have prayed for a long time and are facing challenges like never
before, this book will help you! It has a special word for you and is filled
with revelation knowledge from the Holy Spirit. And one of the greatest
benefits of all, this book will give you a deeper commitment to pray! It

will motivate you to find the time for prayer that God desires, regardless of the demands of your lifestyle.

I read *Don't Leave God Alone* while traveling in South Africa. It gave me such a lift and inspired me so dramatically that I could not put it down. Although I've pressed into God my entire Christian life, I was so stirred by this book that I read it all in one day. When I preached that night, I was *still* energized from what I had read earlier! This book impressed me to press into God like never before.

I want to challenge you to read *Don't Leave God Alone*. It will have a long-term ripple effect on your life and will give you the *push* your life needs to hold on to God until He blesses you!

—Dr. Marilyn Hickey
President, Marilyn Hickey Ministries
Founding Pastor, Orchard Road Christian Center

It Is Not Good for God to Be Alone

The Lord looked down from heaven upon the children of men, to see if there were any that did understand, and seek God.

—Psalm 14:2

Don't leave! Please don't leave!" were the words that stopped me in my tracks as I reached for the door to leave my prayer and study room. I slowly took my hand off the door handle, surprised by what I heard from the gentle voice inside my heart.

"What?" Stunned by His words, I turned around, moving away from the door. "Did You say something to me, Lord?" My heart started beating faster as I realized I had just heard an incredible cry from the heart of God. I said, "Lord, I didn't know You felt that way." I was amazed at the way the Lord was longing for me to stay with Him.

I returned to where I was previously praying to spend more time with God, but my mind was also on the many things I had on my agenda for the day. Couldn't the Lord see my schedule and how much I had to do? Didn't He know I only had an hour of prayer time available—and that prayer time was now over? I began to make excuses as to why I couldn't stay, until I started to sense the Lord's disappointment.

Finally I said, "Father, You really don't want to be left alone, do You?"

I heard Him speak to me again, saying, "No, I don't want to be alone. I was enjoying My time with you, son. And I want to spend more time with you today. You touched My heart, and there are many things I want to talk with someone about today."

"What, Lord?" I replied. "You mean *You* want to talk to *me*?" I was humbled that God was asking me not to leave. Maybe this was what Moses thought when he, being called a friend, talked face-to-face with God. Exodus 33:11 says, "And the LORD spake unto Moses face to face, as a man speaketh unto his friend." I believe God wanted to be with Moses and didn't want to end their time of fellowship together.

I wonder if God ever said similar words to Moses. I can almost hear them: "Moses, don't leave. I want to stay with you." That morning I saw how deeply God wants our fellowship. The scripture at the beginning of this chapter, Psalm 14:2, reveals that the heart of God is literally looking around the earth for anyone who will find the time to seek Him.

PRAYERLESSNESS: LEAVING GOD ALONE

That day forever changed my life by helping me understand that prayer is special to God and cannot be taken lightly. It is so easy in today's fast-paced society to get distracted until our much-needed time with God is lost.

After my experience with God that morning, I realized there is a great danger facing us all right now. The danger is that many Christians don't pray, or they are fighting to maintain what little time they do have to pray.

One of the greatest sins in the church is not necessarily gossip, strife, addictions, adultery, or fornication—even though all of these things are sin. What I believe is the greatest sin today, especially in America, is the sin of prayerlessness or *leaving God alone.*

We can easily become caught in the trap where our only consistent time of prayer is offered before each meal and that's about it. You know what I mean by the *meal prayers*, don't you? I have prayed quite a few of those. It is one we memorize: "God is good; God is great. I'm so hungry I could eat this plate." I've been so hungry before that sometimes I have felt like eating the plate.

One time when I prayed a quick prayer over my meal, I felt the Lord say, "Now, Hank, did you mean that from your heart?" Like most of us, I didn't mean or even hear what I had prayed. Since then, I always feel convicted when I pray insincere prayers, even if the food is making my mouth water.

Prayer, however, is about so much more than that. The truth is that we need a deep commitment to prayer that goes far beyond our meals. Additionally, it is far more than praying only when problems arise. I have found prayer becomes easy when you are in some kind of trouble. It seems like you have more energy to reach out to God when you need an answer to a difficult situation. But God wants our time consistently, regardless of what circumstances are present in our lives.

The way to develop this type of personal relationship with God—the kind that moves His heart—is to set a time and a place to meet Him. The Lord looks forward to your special set time together. You can become determined to not leave God alone by developing a consistent prayer habit. Give God the desire of His heart—He wants to be with you, to spend time with you. Be committed to it until the habit takes a permanent hold in your life.

Talk to the Lord about your desire to be with Him. By verbalizing your commitment, you remind yourself that to have a fruitful walk with God, you must find devoted time to fellowship with Him. Imagine what would happen. If we would refuse to leave God alone that way, miraculous things would begin to take place.

LEAVING GOD ALONE IS RISKY BUSINESS

The Lord is, and always will be, the answer to every problem. We need Him involved in our lives every day. I remember how uncertain we all felt after 9/11. The only thing we could depend on was the Lord. All of a sudden, churches and prayer meetings were packed. People everywhere were trying to sort out their own confusion. They began calling on God in unprecedented numbers. There seemed to be a renewed hunger for and a dependence on the Lord.

The Bible teaches us that during prosperous times, men tend to forget the Lord. But when trouble strikes, they run to Him. This is what happened with 9/11. People ran to the Lord—but it only lasted for a short time.

This type of spiritual lifestyle is risky business. I believe by seeking God only when trouble comes, we live on a dangerous edge. People do it because they see Jesus as the Savior, but they aren't committed to making Him their Lord. They are content to seek Him only when things go badly. The remainder of the time they would rather run the risk of waiting for the next misfortune than commit to God regularly.

One day I was watching the war on television, the same day the American troops seized Baghdad after only twenty-one days. Then a few years later, while I was again watching the war, the events were completely different. We went from a clean sweep into Baghdad to many soldiers dying and violence everywhere.

What was the difference? I believe it was because many people stopped praying for our men and women serving in the military. We left God alone on the matter, and, without the needed prayer coverage, the lives of our men and women in military service were at risk. We felt a mandate of prayer at the beginning of the war. Then later it became less of a concern and perhaps played a large part as to why good results in the war became less visible.

If we want to go higher in the spirit, we cannot let tragedy be our motivation for prayer. Instead, it has to be a hunger for fellowship with God.

Going without regular communion with the Lord becomes risky business when we go astray from His protective hand. Remember, there is safety in regular prayer and a daily commitment to God.

THE HUNGER OF ONE MAN

And it came to pass, that, as he was praying in a certain place, when he ceased, one of his disciples said unto him, Lord, teach us to pray, as John also taught his disciples.

—Luke 11:1

In this verse, the question this disciple asked was about prayer. The man didn't say, "Lord, teach us to prophesy, evangelize, or even perform miracles." The emphasis was on prayer. He was the only person hungry enough to ask about it. Yet in Jesus's ministry, many of the multitudes were hungry, but hungrier for their physical needs.

Have you noticed that when Jesus fed the multitudes, nobody left? Five thousand men plus women and children stayed around. Yet when He called for prayer, the numbers got smaller. Does that sound a little familiar?

Being the pastor of a church, I have noticed that when you call for midweek pizza, a fellowship meal, or even a Super Bowl party, a lot of people show up. The midweek prayer meetings in most churches, however, have a smaller commitment.

God wants us to develop a new kind of hunger—a spiritual hunger. The disciple spoken about in Luke 11:1 had that kind of hunger. He recognized that the key to success in life is found in prayer.

Alone With God, You Learn to Pray

If you will commit yourself to prayer, you will learn the secrets to a powerful prayer life. I have learned the most about prayer by staying with it no matter how I felt or what the present circumstance.

Once again using the disciple in Luke 11:1 as our example, if you ask Jesus how to pray, He will teach you. Much of my learning about prayer came from just getting alone with God. When you get alone with the Lord, He *will* teach you—if you are determined to learn.

After the disciple asked Jesus to teach him to pray, did you notice that Jesus didn't hesitate? For the next twelve verses, He taught a detailed session on prayer. He kept it simple, breaking it down into three general categories that give us the basic makeup needed for a successful prayer life:

1. Personal prayer for you (verses 2–4)
2. Prayer for others (verses 5–9)
3. Persistence in prayer (verses 10–13)

If you include each of these throughout your various times with God, you will begin with a well-rounded life of prayer.

We do not have to make powerful prayer complicated. After more than twenty years of serving God, I keep it simple. I make God real to me. He is real to me. And the more real I make Jesus, the more real He becomes in my life.

Just get alone with the Lord, and He will teach you to pray. Don't become discouraged if some of your prayer times with the Lord feel dry or unproductive. Begin with a hunger to spend time with Him, and the Holy Spirit will help you succeed.

THE GOOD, BAD, AND UGLY

The mountain, the valley, and the desert are all places we will face at some point in our lives.

There are those mountaintop experiences when everything is good. The desert times of our lives are the badlands, when everything feels dry—so dry it seems like when you pray, puffs of dust come from your mouth. Finally, the valley is when you feel low and hopeless. The valley is an ugly place—when God seems a million miles away and problems are looming above you. Like me, I am sure you have experienced all of these at one time or another. Remember, Jesus did too!

Jesus's prayer life shows us that we can maintain consistent prayer in every type of circumstance. First, we know of three separate times a day that He prayed. The Bible says He spent many mornings, some afternoons, and evenings with God. His example reveals that He was committed to prayer.

Successful prayer in every circumstance, again, starts with commitment. The following scriptures show us the unwavering commitment of Jesus's prayer life.

- He prayed in the morning: "And in the morning, rising up a great while before day, he went out, and departed into a solitary place, and there prayed" (Mark 1:35).

- He prayed in the afternoon: "When he had sent the multitudes away, he went up into a mountain apart to pray: and when the evening was come, he was there alone" (Matthew 14:23).

- He prayed in the evening: "He went out into a mountain to pray, and continued all night in prayer to God" (Luke 6:12).

Secondly, Jesus prayed regardless of the situation surrounding Him. He prayed in the same types of situations we sometimes face. He prayed in the mountains, in the wilderness, and in the valley. He conquered these areas in prayer, giving us the hope to also be victorious over them.

If Jesus could pray in the valley, you can pray in the valley—and find your victory! Because Jesus prayed in the wilderness where it was hot and dry, you too can pray and connect with God in the dry desert times. And since He also prayed on the mountain, it reminds us that even when everything around us is wonderful, we have to stay committed to prayer.

Jesus's example of prayer reveals that we can stay close to God in prayer no matter what situations we face or what kind of schedule we keep. Determination to pray whether life is good, bad, or even downright ugly sometimes is a milestone of victory to cross.

Many people can only pray successfully when everything is going well. It is not good to leave God alone just because the scenery changes or circumstances don't conform to a comfortable environment. Committed prayer, regardless of your circumstances, will promote you in the kingdom.

Oh, Deer and a Sack Full of Snacks

I remember a time when I felt both the valley and the desert at the same time. It seemed like years, but it really only lasted about six months.

God seemed as if He was on vacation and somehow forgot about me. Prayer felt boring. I had had enough of being continually disappointed from not sensing God's presence, falling asleep in prayer, and not seeing any answers to my prayers. So I decided to get away to a camp and spend three days fasting and praying. I must admit, I brought a sack full of snacks just in case this valley and time of drought that I was in continued while I was there.

After arranging my cabin the way I wanted, I decided to walk through the nearby woods. I felt alone and, quite honestly, felt like I was just wasting my time. I saw some deer in a field just off in the distance and thought of the scripture that says, "As the deer pants for the water brooks, so pants my soul for You, O God" (Psalm 42:1, NKJV). So I said, "Lord, if You are hearing me, make those deer come close to me."

You know what happened? As God is my witness, those deer ran in the opposite direction!

There I stood alone and presumed that God also wanted to be alone because I felt like He was nowhere to be found. I shook my fist in the air and said, "God, I have had enough!" And then I began to do what many of us do: I began to tell God how to do His job.

"Lord," I said, "if I were You, I would have had those deer come to me. But then, I'm not You." So instead of going back to the cabin to eat my snacks, I decided to first lie down on the ground to rest—but I fell asleep. I awoke about forty-five minutes later to a strange sound. That's when I noticed the deer just a few feet away.

I couldn't believe my eyes. The Lord must have been listening after all.

Thrilled, I went back to my cabin, and for the first time in months, I felt His presence and heard His voice. I didn't eat the snacks after all, but I had a great time with Him.

The Lord taught me a lesson during that time of prayer. He told me that He wanted me to pursue Him, even in the driest times, because if I could maintain that level of perseverance, something would be built in me that could not be taken away. I learned that praying, regardless of what you *feel* like, will eventually pay off if you stay with it.

Perseverance in prayer is what made Jesus's prayer life so successful. In Luke 6:12, Jesus went to a mountain and prayed all night long. Notice the results:

And He came down with them and stood on a level place with a crowd of His disciples and a great multitude of people from all Judea and Jerusalem, and from the seacoast of Tyre and Sidon, who came to hear Him and be healed of their diseases, as well as those who were tormented with unclean spirits. And they were healed. And the whole multitude sought to touch Him, for power went out from Him and healed them all.

—Luke 6:17–19, NKJV

After He spent time praying in a desert wilderness, multitudes of people were healed and delivered. Like Jesus, when we determine to pray through the dry times, the valley times, or even during good mountain experiences, God will always meet our needs and manifest His power.

MY HOUSE IS CALLED A HOUSE OF PRAYER

And he went into the temple, and began to cast out them that sold therein, and them that bought; saying unto them, It is written, My house is the house of prayer: but ye have made it a den of thieves.

—Luke 19:45–46

What was His house called? He called it the house of prayer. When God calls something by a name, does He mean it? Yes, of course He does!

Think about it; of all the things He could call His house or church, He called it the house of *prayer*. He did not call it the house of evangelism. He did not call it the house of praise and worship, or the house of teaching, or the house of deliverance. He did not even call it the house of the prophetic or the apostolic. His house wasn't about just looking good, having new programs, or even making great television. All of those things have a place and are important, but what did He call His house? He called it the house of *prayer*.

Again, how important is it when God calls something by a particular name? Think about the Holy Spirit, the third person of the Trinity. What is He called? He is called the *Holy* Spirit. We know that He is a *worthy* spirit. He is also a *teaching* Spirit, and He is the Spirit of *grace*.

Yes, He is all of these things. But it's important to remember what He is *called*—the *Holy* Spirit.

The word *holy* is obviously the most important description for Him. In heaven, the only thing the Bible records that the angels around the throne of God never cease to say about the Lord is "holy, holy, holy." It is because *this is* the main characteristic or attribute that God wants us to know about His Spirit. So when Jesus said His house should be called a house of prayer, even though it has many attributes, we have to realize that this was the main one He wanted us to see.

Have you ever looked at church listings in the phone book to see how many churches in your own city have prayer services offered during the week? I decided to do a little research to find out. I was looking for churches that advertise prayer as a regular part of their ministry schedule. What I found was that many churches in America hardly have a prayer service at all. They don't have a midweek prayer service or even some type of daily prayer time for the prayer team. Many substituted a prayer service with a midweek meal and short teaching.

Talking with a few pastors, I found that many just resorted to removing scheduled prayer because the attendance was so low. They were tired of holding prayer meetings for only a few people. It seems like there are more and more churches doing that now.

Many people, including pastors, have substituted prayer with other programs and preferences. Perhaps there is a connection between our prayer commitment and the lack of miracles in the church today. Acts 6:2–4 tells us that during the days of the early church, the apostles were found in the Word of God and in prayer. They allowed others to do the functional things of ministry. Today ministers have to deal with so many distractions that can keep them from the Word of God and prayer; thus the Holy Spirit is not able to move more powerfully.

When Jesus said His house was called the house of prayer, He was serious. He wants prayer to take center stage in our churches so we can enjoy the power of God in them. Creating a house of prayer means more than just training a few intercessors; it means the whole church needs to become involved. In other words, everyone needs to have the attitude that they will attend prayer services so God can shake cities and nations.

Prayer is the foundation of everything we do as Christians, corporately and individually. Your church will be more successful if you decide you will not leave God alone by attending your church's prayer meeting. We can all help our churches rise to the next level of prayer by supporting the pastors in our prayer commitment. If you do, it will enable the Lord to use you as a blessing in your church.

Once I was preaching in a larger church that appeared to have a lot of great things happening. But I noticed something: like many churches—including my own sometimes—attention to prayer was less a priority than the other departments in the church. People were so involved in other things that there was just no time left for the church to pray together.

Today we need praying churches that will decide it is just not good to leave God alone in prayer. Then we can fulfill the title Jesus gave His house when He called it a house of prayer.

HOUSE OF PRAYER OR DEN OF THIEVES

It is written, My house is the house of prayer: but ye have made it a den of thieves.

—Luke 19:46

Notice here that even though Jesus called His house a house of prayer, men made it something else. They created a den of thieves instead. Whether it is the church house or our individual house, Jesus is looking for it to be a house of prayer.

Why do you suppose He saw a den of thieves replacing that in this verse? It is because other things were stealing prayer from His house. The reason individuals and churches lack the supernatural is because they do not create a house-of-prayer environment. We are left with only a den of thieves when we allow other priorities to steal the place of prayer.

The Lord is so hungry for our time that He wants nothing to take its place. It is so much on His mind to be with us that He created patterns for us to follow so we will stay on track with it.

He knows the devil has many strategically placed distractions to implement a den of thieves in our lives. Satan wants us to harden our hearts to the importance of prayer by deceiving us into changing the way God designed it to work.

Isn't that the way it happens? God sets a pattern or a standard, but men change it. Eventually the truth of what God says is lost. The Pharisees did the same thing in Matthew 15:4–9. They changed the truth of what God said. Jesus pointed it out. He said there were three specific ways in which the Pharisees had changed the truth of God. Jesus said, "*They* made," "*They* did," and "*They* said." Who made, did, and said? It was not God; it was they—the Pharisees. They did their own thing, contrary to what the Lord commanded.

This is how many make excuses regarding God's house of prayer. They might say things like, "I know it's to be called the house of prayer, but I am too busy," or "Prayer is not really my thing." Others will tell you that churches with a serious prayer commitment are a little too extreme for their taste or their lifestyle.

The Bible doesn't say that. It says His house shall be called a *house of prayer.*

Remember Jesus is Lord of the church, and He can call His church whatever He wants. What right do we have to change it? We should be excited to do exactly what Jesus says and not to *make, do,* or *say* something—anything—else.

There are things that will steal from the house of prayer, and before we know it, we find ourselves creating excuses for them. This might include staying up too late at night, ultimately making you too tired for prayer in the morning. Correcting that means we may not be able to watch some midnight television shows, and we might have to leave late-night snacks for rare occasions.

A life dedicated to consistent prayer is obviously something we need to fight for. Think for a moment; what things are stealing your house of prayer today? It will help you avoid the den of thieves that tempts us all to make excuses for our prayer life. It is easy to become too busy for prayer—without even realizing it has happened. Consistency of not leaving God alone in prayer will create stability and blessing in your life.

THE BODY ON THE INTERSTATE

After two decades of serving the Lord, I have learned the importance of a daily pursuit of God. Many years ago, I was faced with a situation where I could only depend on my established relationship with the Lord. That relationship paid off.

We had just been at church, and I dropped the guest speaker off at the airport. It was late at night, and I was on the interstate driving back home. There was little traffic and I was in the car worshiping the Lord for the powerful service we just had. Suddenly I saw a car with its flashers on sitting in the middle of the interstate. And there was a man lying on the highway.

With very little time to think, I slammed on my brakes and pulled over to the side of the road. When I got out of the car, I was met by a marine. He told me that the man lying on the road had just been hit by a car while trying to run across the highway. I told him that I was a pastor and wanted to help. We decided it was best for him to guide traffic while I attended to the driver who hit the man. He was visibly upset and shaken while the victim lay bleeding in a fetal position on the ground.

The driver was crying and hunched over the victim, whom his car had just hit at a high rate of speed. The impact had been so hard that part of the victim's hair remained in the grille of the car. The driver had been going the speed limit, but he couldn't see the young man attempting to cross the highway in the dark.

I knelt down next to the bleeding young man. His head was so swollen and bleeding I couldn't make out many of his features, even with the headlights of the car shining down at him. It was a miracle that he was even alive and breathing.

Immediately I put my hands on him, called out to God, and prayed in the spirit. Then I started to prophesy to him. I commanded life to come into him and said that not any of his bones would be broken. I commanded a miracle for this young man. He started to cough as I prayed, and he let out a small moan.

I could hear the weak sound of his voice, and I asked if he could hear me. I told him I was a pastor, that everything was going to be OK, and God would perform a miracle for him. I wanted to make sure he was saved, so I encouraged him to call on Jesus. He weakly repeated after me to ask Jesus into his heart.

The presence and power of God was so strong. The rescue workers even allowed me to continue praying as they arrived on the scene and did their work. I told the ambulance crew that God was going to do a miracle for this young man and not one bone would be broken.

Later at the hospital, the rescue workers, the medical staff, and the marine couldn't believe what happened. They all agreed that it was indeed a miracle. The doctors said it was amazing that not one of the young man's bones were broken. Glory to God! They said he should have been dead.

They allowed me to see the young man, and he thanked me for praying for him. He told me, "At first I thought you were an angel because you kept saying my name."

Honestly, I don't ever remember saying his name. Perhaps as I prayed in the spirit, God called out to him. He also heard the prophetic word that he would live and not one of his bones would be broken. Later he visited the church and was living proof to the congregation of a walking miracle.

I thank God that a lifestyle of prayer paid off for that young man. When you don't leave God alone, you can be confident to trust that, no matter what the circumstances, He will be there for you when you need Him most.

RUN TO GOD, NOT THE FIG LEAF

Of course, sometimes choosing not to leave God alone is easier said than done. As determined as I am about prayer, the den of thieves just doesn't want to go away easily.

Too often we find ourselves failing in this area again and again. The natural response for many Christians is to give up when they feel they have let God down in prayer. They would rather avoid it than face failure again. They think God is too angry with them or they are embarrassed, so now they run away from prayer—they run away from God. But be encouraged because there is hope for all of us.

Adam and Eve experienced a similar feeling. In Genesis 3, God walked in the cool of the day, looking for His regular time of fellowship with His friends—this is the same way He craves fellowship with you too. On this occasion, however, they had sinned against the Lord by eating from the tree that God had told them was off-limits. They immediately chose to hide from the presence of the Lord and to cover themselves.

This was another form of leaving God alone. Do you know why they did it?

They went from being *un*ashamed to feeling a new sense of embarrassment for what they had done. They were used to walking with God and being clothed with His presence, even though physically they had always been naked.

Suddenly they felt exposed and realized they had no clothing on. This new feeling of shame made them want to hide from God and look for another covering. The coverings they chose were fig leaves that they sewed together. Now this fig leaf was their covering, and it stood between them and God's presence.

When people sin, or compromise, they usually don't want to be near God. They feel embarrassed. They feel safer hiding behind a "fig leaf" because they don't want God to see their "nakedness."

Fig leaves are our own effort toward righteousness that we use to help us feel justified in our actions. We can never approach God in our own righteousness or our own works. He will never be impressed with the fig leaves we put together to stand between His presence and us.

When you feel like you have failed or left God alone, don't run from Him; run straight to Him again. Because of the blood of Jesus, your sins are covered, so you don't need to depend on a fig leaf. Depend on His blood to cover you.

When we choose to skip prayer or just find ourselves caught in the distractions of life, we usually find ourselves sewing some fig leaves together, don't we? God wants us to be open with Him and not make any excuses. He wants to help you succeed, even when you have failed. Keep going back to Him for help. By taking this simple step, by continuing to make it a part of your life, before you know it, you *will* be consistent in not leaving Him alone.

Now there are two important reasons why you and I should avoid the fig-leaf remedy. We find them in this account of scripture:

> And Jesus entered into Jerusalem, and into the temple: and when he had looked round about upon all things, and now the eventide was come, he went out unto Bethany with the twelve. And on the morrow, when they were come from Bethany, he was hungry: And seeing a fig tree afar off having leaves, he came, if haply he might find any thing thereon: and when he came to it, he found nothing

but leaves; for the time of figs was not yet. And Jesus answered and
said unto it, No man eat fruit of thee hereafter for ever.

—Mark 11:11–14

The first reason we should avoid a fig-tree remedy is because there is
no fruit in it. Jesus cursed the fig tree.

Why did He curse it?

First, I believe it prophetically represented the same fig leaves Adam
and Eve wore to replace God's presence. When Jesus saw the fig tree,
He found that it bore no fruit. The fig-leaf remedy that Adam and Eve
depended on produced no fruit for them either.

In the same way, we cannot depend on a fig leaf to cover our failures.
Eventually we will realize it is a fruitless effort. The best way is to always
go back to God—no matter what. That is where He can minister to you
and change you from failure in prayer to consistency and success.

Secondly, we want to avoid the fig-leaf remedy because the fig leaf also
represented man's methods replacing God's methods. In verse 11, notice
Jesus was walking around and observing things in the temple. Shortly
after, in verse 12, He sees the fig tree bearing no fruit. I believe Jesus
observing the temple and cursing the fig tree are connected because,
right after He cursed the fig tree, He went back to the temple and threw
out the money changers and the people who were selling doves.

Again, this is no coincidence. Similar to this, many people "sell doves"
by replacing the Holy Spirit's anointing with their own methods.

In other accounts of Jesus cleansing the temple, He also threw out
those who sold oxen and sheep—they speak of serving and of people.
The oxen speak of serving because they are working animals, while sheep
speak of people because Jesus refers to His people as sheep. Why did He
remove them? It was not because serving in the church or the people
themselves are bad. What Jesus wanted to remove was man's replace-
ment of God's presence with his own methods.

Every one of us has to realize that the fig-leaf remedy will never work. It will always leave us with no fruit and only a substitute for the presence of God. Problems arise when we allow substitutes for God's presence. As a result, there is little to no fruit produced. We are then left with nothing but lifeless religion. God does not want that for us. Therefore His way—God's way—of doing things is the only way to go.

ARE YOU LEAVING GOD ALONE?

We have been created for fellowship. We need to do a regular examination of our commitment and pursuit of God. Are we a one-time follower, part-time follower, or even just a casual acquaintance? Or can we say we are His true friends?

A true example of friendship with God is found while Jesus was dying on the cross between two thieves (Luke 23:39–43). One of the robbers wanted Jesus to remember him, and he acknowledged who Jesus was to him personally. As a result, Jesus gave him the promise of paradise.

The other thief pressed Jesus for a miracle, but he had no desire to know Him. This thief represents those who demand that God work for them but who never really want to know Him or receive Him.

When the thief reached out to Jesus, Jesus reached back. When we reach out to God—regardless of the circumstance or even in the middle of our own failures—we will find that God is excited to reach back to us. He wants to fellowship with us. He wants to spend time with us. We must show Him that we want that fellowship too. We just have to refuse to leave Him alone.

We can see the rewards of life are only found when we include Him on more than just a casual basis. The blessings of it are without limit. Never doubt that God wants to be with you. He craves your time, your attention, your fellowship, and your friendship—so I encourage you, don't leave Him alone.

2

WHEN GOD SAID, "LEAVE ME ALONE"

And the LORD said to Moses, "Go, get down! For your people whom you brought out of the land of Egypt have corrupted themselves. They have turned aside quickly out of the way which I commanded them. They have made themselves a molded calf, and worshiped it and sacrificed to it, and said, 'This is your god, O Israel, that brought you out of the land of Egypt!'" And the LORD said to Moses, "I have seen this people, and indeed it is a stiff-necked people! Now therefore, let Me alone, that My wrath may burn hot against them and I may consume them. And I will make of you a great nation." Then Moses pleaded with the LORD his God, and said: "LORD, why does Your wrath burn hot against Your people whom You have brought out of the land of Egypt with great power and with a mighty hand? Why should the Egyptians speak, and say, 'He brought them out to harm them, to kill them in the mountains, and to consume them from the face of the earth'? Turn from Your fierce wrath, and relent from this harm to Your people. Remember Abraham, Isaac, and Israel, Your servants, to whom You swore by Your own self, and said to them, 'I will multiply your descendants as the stars of heaven; and all this land that I have spoken of I give to your descendants, and they shall inherit it forever.'" So the LORD relented from the harm which He said He would do to His people.

—Exodus 32:7–14, NKJV

L EAVE ME ALONE!" were the shocking words that rang in the ears of Moses. The God who loved His people and wanted their fellowship was suddenly saying, "Leave Me alone."

Imagine such words echoing through creation and even in the very bowels of hell itself: *Leave Me alone! Leave Me alone! Leave Me alone!*

I am sure the devil was elated at the sound of those words. In fact, this would mean death to all who followed Moses into the wilderness. This would be a reason for hell to celebrate. I suppose demons celebrate with deviled ham and deviled eggs and, of course, finish the celebration with devil's food cake—right? Not really. I'm just joking.

This is exactly what the enemy wants: for every person to leave God alone and for God to leave all of the people alone. When God and man are separated, the devil gains access to man on Earth in order to kill, steal, and destroy.

The party in the belly of hell, however, was soon interrupted by a different sound. The devil would not be able to carry out his plans after all. The words to follow God's statement of "Leave Me alone" were about to strike fear in hell.

The words came from Moses, in Exodus 32:11: "And Moses besought the Lord..." Another version of that scripture says, "Moses pleaded with the Lord his God..." (NKJV). In other words, Moses was *not* going to leave the Lord alone! The devil didn't want to hear that sound. But Moses was not going to accept no for an answer.

God is always looking for someone in the earth who will refuse to let Him get away. He looks for those who will continue pursuing Him until situations change. The devil hates it when his plans are interrupted and man and God connect through prayer.

> And [God] saw that there was no man, and wondered that there was no intercessor.
>
> —Isaiah 59:16

> And there is none that calleth upon thy name, that stirreth up himself to take hold of [God].
>
> —Isaiah 64:7

As these verses in Isaiah state, God is actually looking to connect with us so He can intervene in our lives. I am convinced that we could have lives that are more abundant if we would seek the Lord every day. The plan of the devil is to keep man and God separated. We know that Jesus's death on the cross made it so that there is no longer a separation between God and man, but *prayerlessness* will re-create it. Hebrews 4:16 says we can now come boldly to the throne of grace and find help and mercy in the time of our need.

Perhaps for just a moment there seemed to be a separation between God and Moses—when God requested to be alone. But Moses stood up and refused to leave the Lord alone until He changed His mind. You can read the account in Exodus 32:14, which says, "So the LORD changed His mind about the harm which He said He would do to His people" (NAS).

Moses changed God's mind? Is that possible?

Yes. This one man changed God's mind, and you can too!

God's mind was changed and Satan's plan was interrupted all because someone refused to leave God alone. The most amazing things can happen when we connect with God and refuse to leave Him alone as Moses did.

DEAD BY 4:00 P.M.

"Dead by 4:00 p.m." I couldn't believe what I had just said to my distressed friend on the phone.

"What?" my friend replied. "Did you say dead by 4:00 p.m. today?"

"That's right," I said. I was speaking about their elderly relative in the hospital who lay in a coma, unresponsive to touch or sound. I told my friend that I had heard the Lord say the person would die at 4:00 p.m. that very day.

"What? She can't die at 4:00 p.m. today because she doesn't know Jesus and has never asked Him to be her Lord and Savior."

Finally, after trying to calm my friend, I heard what I believed to be the instructions of the Lord. I told her, "You need to get everyone out of the room, including the medical staff. Then when you are alone, tell your relative to wake up in Jesus's name. When she awakens, you need to share the gospel with her before 4:00 p.m." The life of this precious soul was hanging in the balance. God knew she was about to slip into eternity without Him if someone didn't intervene.

A few hours had passed since my original conversation with my friend, and I waited, expecting to hear some news. I answered the phone again to hear her irate, wanting an explanation of why her relative didn't wake up. "Well," I said, "did you do what I mentioned? Did you get everyone out of the room and command her to wake up?"

"Well, I kind of did. I got most people out except for a few of my family."

I thought for a minute. Then I said, "The instructions were for *everyone* to leave. You need to get everyone out and try it again."

Later that afternoon they called with a report. This time I heard my friend rejoicing on the other line. I could hardly believe it myself. They were explaining to me how they went back and told everyone to leave for a moment. My friend prayed for the woman who was in a coma and, surprisingly, she woke up.

Not only did she wake up, but she also received Jesus into her heart. She was saved, and, you guessed it, she died by about 4:00 p.m. The good news is: she went to be with Jesus!

You know, I was just as surprised as anyone at these events. But what would happen if we would not have prayed because the situation seemed hopeless? Moses could have given up when God seemed like He was not responding. How many times do we give up when it seems as if nothing is changing in our situation? This friend of mine and I decided that God was going to do a miracle even though it looked at first like God was not going to intervene. Thank God that the devil's plan to steal a precious life was thwarted and, like Moses, we refused to leave God alone.

DON'T CHANGE HIS WORD, CHANGE HIS MIND

We must understand the awesome authority and power we have been given through Jesus Christ. We can never change God's Word because it is forever settled in heaven. Psalm 119:89 says, "For ever, O LORD, thy word is settled in heaven."

Even though God's written Word cannot be changed, we can change God's mind. What I mean is this: we can change God's mind about the outcome of a situation or event, even though it was created by our wrong choices.

God looks for someone to intervene and change the course. This is what Moses did for Israel. He stopped God's pronounced judgment that the children of Israel created for themselves. His persistent faith in God's promised mercy gave God a justified reason to change course. I also believe this is what happened in the story of my friend's relative. We didn't leave God alone and mercy intervened.

In John 14:13, Jesus said, "And whatsoever ye shall ask in my name, that will I do, that the Father may be glorified in the Son." This verse tells us that we can move God simply by asking in Jesus's name. In another place in Scripture, we are told that we can actually command the hands of God. Isaiah 45:11 says, "Thus saith the LORD, the Holy One of Israel, and his Maker, Ask me of things to come concerning my sons, and concerning the work of my hands command ye me."

God wants us to come to Him so circumstances can change. One main reason people are not persistent with God about what they need from Him is because they are always afraid God is mad at them. This was the exact situation with Moses when God said He wanted to be left alone. God *was* angry with the people. Moses, however, persisted anyhow.

When God was angry with them after they worshiped the golden calf, He was ready to wipe them out. Not only did they worship the cow, but they also called it their god and gave it the credit for delivering them from Egypt.

In Exodus 32:5, Aaron called the cow *the Lord*. And Exodus 32:8 says, "They have turned aside quickly out of the way which I commanded them: they have made them a molten calf, and have worshipped it, and have sacrificed thereunto, and said, These be thy gods, O Israel, which have brought thee up out of the land of Egypt."

What a low blow! God was not happy, to say the least. I know I may eat like a cow at times, but I agree with God: I don't want to be mistaken for one!

The worship of this golden beef was enough to put God over the top in His righteous anger. It's no wonder He said, "Leave Me alone!" He was so righteously angry that He was ready to wipe them all out. And He had every right to do so. Thank goodness for Moses's persistence. He pressed God until God changed His mind about what He was going to do.

Do you think that God really wanted to wipe out the children of Israel?

Truthfully, I don't think so. I don't think God was having a pity party either. I especially don't think that the angel Gabriel had to come down and ask God what was wrong. I am certain that God did not have it in His mind to barbecue them in the desert.

Now if Moses could cause God to change His mind under such circumstances, how much more do you think you and I can do it? When God was angry, Moses trusted in His mercy. Now we have the blood of Jesus extending the mercy of God to us.

People too often believe God is always mad at them, so they are not confident to approach Him about anything. I have often noticed that when some people tell stories of times when they have seen a vision of the Lord, it always seems God arrives in an angry or serious demeanor. I know there *may* be those times, but it seems you hardly ever hear about the Lord coming in a vision and smiling. Think about it: people always think of God as being mad. Whenever anything goes wrong, they blame God. Insurance companies call catastrophes "acts of God." Some think it was God who took their loved one's life or put fatal diseases on them to teach them something.

We must always remember: God is a good God—He is good to all! Psalm 145:9 says, "The LORD is good to all: and his tender mercies are over all his works." Acts 10:38 also tells us, "How God anointed Jesus of Nazareth with the Holy Ghost and with power: who went about doing good, and healing all that were oppressed of the devil; for God was with him."

Change your thinking that God is always angry with you. We find that Jesus came for the purpose of doing good and showing mercy. God wants us to come to Him and be persistent. He is looking for someone who will ask for His intervention and mercy. When God said, "Leave Me alone," to Moses, I believe it was as if He was looking over His shoulder, waiting to see what Moses would do on behalf of the people. If Moses would stand up for the people, then God was bound by His covenant with them to do the same. If Moses, being only a man, could find a reason for God to show His mercy, then how much more does God want to give it?

THE NATION OF ... MOSES?

I can just see it now: all maps of the world and all textbooks calling the nation of Israel, the nation of *Moses*. We don't realize just how close Israel was to being named Moses.

Did you ever think of that? Let me explain. The nation of Israel was named after a person in the Bible—Jacob—who would later have his name changed to Israel after being renamed by the Lord. Genesis 32:28 says, "And [God] said, Thy name shall be called no more Jacob, but Israel."

Originally, Israel was the nation of Jacob, in a sense, even though it was not referred to that way. But Jacob became Israel, and when God called him Israel, that also became the name of the nation. Israel was named after this man Jacob.

What would have happened to the name if God had wiped out the people? Had Moses not stood up for the children of Israel, this is exactly what could have happened: in Deuteronomy 9:14, the Bible says, "Let me alone, that I may destroy them, and blot out their name from under heaven: and I will make of thee a nation mightier and greater than they."

God was ready to do away with their entire name. Then He was planning to start over with Moses. We can safely assume that if the people had been destroyed, God would have started a new nation after Moses and named it after him. It is hard to even think along those lines, but this is how determined God was. Still, deep in God's heart, I don't believe He truly wanted the nation of Moses. Instead, God was waiting for a covenant man to stand up and find a reason for Him to extend mercy.

If Moses would have left God alone, then those people would have died because God is righteousness and justice was required for their sins. Yet we have to remember that there are two main characteristics about God: He is *all* righteous, but He is also *all* mercy. These are the two sides of the mercy seat—one side is justice while the other is mercy.

God had to enforce His justice on the sin of the people, but He needed a valid reason to extend His mercy side instead. So Moses stood before God to give Him a reason to show mercy.

If Moses had not stepped up to the challenge, God would have had to start over with Moses. The newly formed children of Israel might have been renamed the children of Moses. We would have had Iraq, Iran, and the nation of Moses. We would be traveling to visit Jerusalem, Moses, instead of Jerusalem, Israel. The news reporters might even report that there was war in Moses today.

I do not believe that was on God's heart to do. Instead, I believe God wanted someone to stand up and plead mercy so His righteous anger would be aborted. When God requested to be left alone, He was really looking for someone who would *not* leave Him alone.

Remember, Moses changed the mind of God, and you can too. Look at Exodus 32:12, where Moses stood up and said, "No, God, You are not going to do this." He said, "Wherefore should the Egyptians speak, and say, For mischief did he bring them out, to slay them in the mountains, and to consume them from the face of the earth? Turn from thy fierce wrath, and repent of this evil against thy people."

Moses was telling God that he was not leaving Him alone until He remembered His agreement with the people. He wasn't going to allow God's anger to keep him from coming to Him about it anyhow.

What would happen if you did the same thing, if all of a sudden you said, "No matter what, I'm not going to leave God alone; I'm going to pray until things change"?

We can do it for ourselves, our families, and our cities and nations. We could actually change the mind of God regarding what has been destined—because of sin—for our nations. We can turn the events in our lives toward blessing.

I used to think that changing God's mind was like asking my dad for the car keys when I was sixteen. No matter how hard I tried to change my dad's mind, I wasn't going to be able to do it because whatever Dad says goes. I used to believe this was the same way with God until I noticed what Moses did. He requested mercy, even when it didn't look like it was going to be given.

Then I saw how Hezekiah did the same thing. When God told him he would die, Hezekiah went before God, and the Lord granted him a fifteen-year extension to his life. When he sought the Lord, he got results. If these people could change the mind of God, then you are no different. God is looking for you to stand up today and do the same.

THE MAN WHO QUIT COUNTING

Not everyone, however, who could have changed God's mind did so. As I mentioned before in this chapter, we know that Moses didn't leave God alone, and as a result, a whole nation was saved. There was a man who chose to leave God alone, however, and the result was two cities destroyed.

> And the LORD went his way, as soon as he had left communing with Abraham: and Abraham returned unto his place.
>
> —Genesis 18:33

> Then GOD rained brimstone and fire down on Sodom and Gomorrah—a river of lava from GOD out of the sky!—and destroyed these cities and the entire plain and everyone who lived in the cities and everything that grew from the ground.
>
> —Genesis 19:24–25, THE MESSAGE

We can see that our persistent prayers make a difference. The destiny of two cities was determined by one man who quit counting and left God alone regarding them.

Just as God didn't want to be left alone regarding Israel, I don't think He wanted to be left alone concerning Sodom and Gomorrah. He was just looking for someone to intervene and pray. We know this because God took the time to speak with Abraham before He destroyed the two cities: "And the Lord said, Shall I hide from Abraham [My friend and servant] what I am going to do" (Genesis 18:17, AMP). If He really wanted to destroy them, He could have done so without saying anything at all to His friend.

Now if Moses prayed for the people and judgment was spared, why didn't the same occur with Abraham and the cities of Sodom and Gomorrah? It is because, unlike Moses, Abraham ultimately left God alone. Verse 33 of Genesis 18 says, "And the LORD went his way..."

If there was ever a time to *not* let God get away, it was then. This was costly on the part of Abraham. What happened with Moses could have happened with Abraham. The people could have been saved by the cry of one man.

Abraham originally began to plead with God, but he gave up too early. We find in Genesis 18 how he began to address God on behalf of the people. He begins by counting numbers with God:

> The men set out for Sodom, but Abraham stood in GOD's path, blocking his way. Abraham confronted him, "Are you serious? Are you planning on getting rid of the good people right along with the bad? What if there are fifty decent people left in the city; will you lump the good with the bad and get rid of the lot? Wouldn't you spare the city for the sake of those fifty innocents? I can't believe you'd do that, kill off the good and the bad alike as if there were no difference between them. Doesn't the Judge of all the Earth judge with justice?"
>
> —Genesis 18:22–25, THE MESSAGE

This story sounds very similar to that of Moses. Abraham began to question God's judgment by trying to locate enough righteous people in order for God to change His mind. God agreed that He would spare the cities for each amount of righteous that Abraham requested. Finally, when they got down to the number ten, Abraham asked God to spare the city if they could find that many righteous.

One day while I was reading this passage, I asked God why He destroyed Sodom and Gomorrah. As quickly as I said that, the Holy Spirit said to me that He didn't have to destroy them. They were destroyed because Abraham stopped at ten. If Abraham had just stood up and said, "God, I refuse to leave You alone for one righteous," he could have changed the mind of God. God was willing to hear the cry of one man, but Abraham stopped counting and *left God alone.*

God was left to go His way, and a city was lost. Remember, Genesis 18:33 says, "And the LORD went his way…" In other words, God went away to be left alone. Then, after God left, Abraham went to his own place.

What if Abraham would have chased God, saying, "Excuse me, but Lord, I know there may not even be ten righteous. What about my nephew Lot? He's over there. Would You spare it for just him?"

Perhaps Sodom and Gomorrah would still be here today because Abraham stood for one righteous man. Perhaps it would have been judged at a later time, but think about it: if one man could change the mind of God when it came to Moses, then how was this any different? It wasn't. The difference was that Abraham quit counting and Moses persisted.

Rather than really wanting to be left alone, God is looking for people who will give Him a reason to intervene even when He is not obligated to do it. When God is declaring that judgment is deserved, He looks for one man who will plead for His mercy. Perhaps when God told Moses to leave Him alone, it was a test to see what Moses would do. Moses's willing response to fight for mercy of an undeserving people meant that God, who was bound by the same covenant, would have to extend mercy also.

Similarly, when God commanded Abraham to sacrifice Isaac, Abraham's willing response meant that God would also have to sacrifice *His* only Son. One man's persistence for God's mercy will cause God to respond. God wants to intervene, but He is looking for people who will stand up and ask Him. He is looking for people who will not leave Him alone until things change.

A Lesson From Miss USA

When the woman who was crowned Miss USA was in danger of losing her crown because of accusations of inappropriate behavior, an incredible thing happened. According to the rules of the organization, she was not upholding the moral standard of such a position. The head of the organization had the power to either fire her or give her a second chance. After a meeting, she was given a second chance. He changed his mind. She clearly violated the policies of being Miss USA and probably didn't deserve it, yet she was given a second chance.

I believe this is a prophetic message for us today. If this organization was willing to be merciful and give her another chance, how much more is God also willing to give the United States and other nations another chance, even though He has every reason to judge them? And even after we have clearly violated His moral standards and deserve judgment. I believe God is looking for every reason to extend mercy to every nation, but He needs someone who will pray.

God gave Israel another chance. He would have given Sodom and Gomorrah one too. He just needs one man or woman who will give Him a just reason to change His mind. The Lord wants someone who will not leave Him alone so He can show His mercy.

Yes, one man truly can change the mind of God. In the case of Nineveh, God purposely sent Jonah to be that man. We find in the story of Jonah that, even though Nineveh deserved judgment, God desperately wanted to show them mercy. He was looking for one man who would give Him a reason not to destroy the city.

Once while I was praying for America, a very interesting thing happened to me. I had my head buried in the couch, asking the Lord for mercy on the United States. I felt an overwhelming presence and started to sense the holy fear that you feel when the Lord's presence is there. It felt as if the Lord was sitting next to me—as near as I could tell. I was too afraid to look.

I felt a warmth of what seemed to be a touch on me, and I heard these words: "I am giving this nation another chance as I gave Nineveh. I still have much to be accomplished. I am not finished yet. Tell people to never forget that I still hold in the palms of My hands the sands that are soaked with the tears of your forefathers' prayers for this nation."

Now I know many are prophesying and even anticipating the destruction of this nation. Not me. I suddenly realized a man, Moses, stood up for the people, and we can too. How much more would my refusal to not leave God alone make a difference? We need to stand up and not leave God alone until we see our heart's desire for our nation come to pass.

THE CRY OF THE RIGHTEOUS

We can see a further truth from Moses and Abraham that the cry of the righteous must always be louder than the cry of evil. If not, evil will always prevail.

Interestingly enough, God initially came down to talk to Abraham because He heard the cry of Sodom and Gomorrah. Genesis 18:20–21 says, "And the LORD said, Because the cry of Sodom and Gomorrah is great, and because their sin is very grievous; I will go down now, and see whether they have done altogether according to the cry of it, which is come unto me; and if not, I will know."

There was a wicked cry coming from the two cities. Therefore God needed Abraham's cry to be louder than the cry of evil in Sodom and Gomorrah. There needed to be a cry for mercy that resounded above that which came from the wicked.

When darkness begins to make a sound, we need to create the sound of the anointing that opposes it. What happens if we remain quiet and leave God alone about our families and never pray for them? Or we leave that rebellious teenager alone and never pray for him or her? What happens if we stay silent about that financial situation and just hope that it works out? The result will be that the sound of the negative situation will probably be louder than the answer.

What happens if we don't pray about sickness when it tries to attack our bodies? Then we will probably stay sick. Whatever we remain silent about, and leave God alone about, He will stay silent about too. Your marriage may be a mess, but are you going to leave God alone about it? People tend to complain in unbelief, but imagine what would happen if we didn't leave God alone about our circumstances.

Well, maybe you have tried that before, but the problem is that you finally let go and gave up. When you make your cry of faith louder than the circumstance that is telling you there is no hope, something will begin to happen. Hold on to God, and don't let go until He blesses you. He always responds to the righteous cry of His people. Look at Psalm 34:15. It says, "GOD keeps an eye on his friends, his ears pick up every moan and groan" (THE MESSAGE). Be assured that when the cry of righteousness is louder than the cry of evil, circumstances change and miracles begin to unfold.

CHANGING GOD'S MIND OVER OUR CITIES AND NATIONS

By not leaving God alone—the same way Moses did and how Abraham should have—we are able to affect cities and nations. Notice in Ezekiel 28 six things that happen when we choose to be silent concerning our cities. These six things are what followed Lucifer when he was cast out of heaven.

By the multitude of thy merchandise they have filled the midst of thee with violence, and thou hast sinned: therefore I will cast thee as profane out of the mountain of God: and I will destroy thee, O covering cherub, from the midst of the stones of fire. Thine heart was lifted up because of thy beauty, thou hast corrupted thy wisdom by reason of thy brightness: I will cast thee to the ground, I will lay thee before kings, that they may behold thee. Thou hast defiled thy sanctuaries by the multitude of thine iniquities, by the iniquity of thy traffick; therefore will I bring forth a fire from the midst of thee, it shall devour thee, and I will bring thee to ashes upon the earth in the sight of all them that behold thee. All they that know thee among the people shall be astonished at thee: thou shalt be a terror, and never shalt thou be any more.

—Ezekiel 28:16–19

Here we see the demonic influence that we are able to stop by persistence and determination with God. If you feel frustrated with the condition of the church, go before the Lord and pray. If you are disturbed by the murder and crime rate in your town, then don't leave God alone until the numbers go down. Look at the demonic influences from Ezekiel 28 that we overcome when we rise up and pray:

1. Violence (verse 16)
2. Profanity (verse 16)
3. Corrupt wisdom (verse 17)
4. Defiled sanctuaries (verse 18)
5. Iniquities (verse 18)
6. Terrorism/fear (verse 19)

If you are tired of seeing things from this list on the news channel, then choose to not leave God alone about them. Think of what can be aborted by not leaving God alone for our cities and nations. No wonder God longs for our involvement with Him on the earth.

In 2004, I was ministering at a conference in Jacksonville, Florida. I remember prophesying that year that Florida would experience two storms, back-to-back hurricanes. The prophetic word went on to say that if we would pray, they would stay out. I know many who did pray the first time, and the hurricanes still came. Our prayers obviously needed to rise to a higher level.

So the next year I prophesied again, including the name of a storm that would rise up out of the Atlantic Ocean in a particular month. I was to be speaking at another conference around that time, and I told the host that the storm would come just before the meeting. This time hundreds of people prayed with fervency. They just decided that this time the storm was not allowed to come in like before. They prayed, and the storm was never able to hit them. What was the difference? I believe people became determined, regardless of the previous circumstance, they were not accepting no for the answer.

In the latter part of 2005, the Lord spoke to my heart that in 2006 we wouldn't have storms like the previous few years. He was putting His feet over the nation and sending the storms out to sea. I know many people after record years of hurricanes have been praying and declaring peace to the storms. As a result, in the year 2006 there were no major hurricanes to hit the United States. Some tried but never succeeded because people all over, collectively, individually, and fervently prayed. There was a great difference when people rose up and did not leave God alone about it.

WHEN I FELT GOD LEAVE ME

I tell you, my friend, the worst thing that could happen is to have a life without God. That is the horror of eternal damnation. It is being forever separated from God. Once, however, years ago, I felt a sense of what it might be like to be without Him. I was ministering at a conference, and some rather well-known people were present in the meeting who had come to hear me speak. I walked up the steps of the stage, feeling confident, and began to preach my message.

Suddenly I found myself changing my message away from what God gave me. I didn't think my original sermon would be along the lines of what they came to hear. I looked out to see if I had their approval while I was preaching. Immediately I sensed something was wrong. I felt the Lord lift His anointing. There I was, standing all alone, without the anointing of the Holy Spirit, in front of all these people. I knew that what I was doing those few minutes had grieved the Lord, and I felt so sick in my heart.

I couldn't wait to get back to my hotel room. When I got back, I opened the door of my room and fell onto the bed weeping. I repented to God for changing His words and trying to please man instead of Him. Thank God, He is so forgiving. But I knew then that I don't ever want Him to leave me.

It is always best to please God rather than man. God wants to be with us, and I realized what it really feels like to be without Him in a situation. I don't want to leave Him alone.

THE LORD DOESN'T WANT TO BE ALONE

We must never forget that God doesn't really want to be alone. The reason He said, "Leave me alone," was to provoke a response from Moses. Even at times when it seemed like the Lord wanted solitude, He was not trying to separate from us. There were times it appeared that Jesus didn't want to be bothered. He even seemed to ignore the needs of some.

Perhaps you have felt the Lord was ignoring your need—when your prayers seemed to be delayed or unanswered. But Jesus wasn't ignoring them. He always looks to provoke a response of determined faith.

When Jesus hung alone on the cross, crying "My God, my God, why hast thou forsaken me?" God seemed to have left Him. God was not unconcerned or uncaring. He wanted to provoke a response from His Son—which was mercy even though God turned away from the sin He saw on Jesus—who was still determined to hang there on the cross anyhow. Yes, Jesus was determined, just like Moses and others who would not leave God alone even when He seemed to request it.

God wasn't ignoring Jesus, and He isn't ignoring you. He is waiting for your response of determination. Sometimes it may seem like the Lord is far away or even hard of hearing, but that is not the case. Instead, God is waiting to provoke a response from you so He can intervene and bless your life.

3

THOSE WHO REFUSED TO
LEAVE GOD ALONE

And what shall I more say? for the time would fail me to tell of Gedeon, and of Barak, and of Samson, and of Jephthae; of David also, and Samuel, and of the prophets: Who through faith subdued kingdoms, wrought righteousness, obtained promises, stopped the mouths of lions, quenched the violence of fire, escaped the edge of the sword, out of weakness were made strong, waxed valiant in fight, turned to flight the armies of the aliens. Women received their dead raised to life again: and others were tortured, not accepting deliverance; that they might obtain a better resurrection: And others had trial of cruel mockings and scourgings, yea, moreover of bonds and imprisonment: They were stoned, they were sawn asunder, were tempted, were slain with the sword: they wandered about in sheepskins and goatskins; being destitute, afflicted, tormented; (of whom the world was not worthy:) they wandered in deserts, and in mountains, and in dens and caves of the earth. And these all, having obtained a good report through faith, received not the promise.

—Hebrews 11:32–39

E'S FALLEN TWELVE feet down from a window," she said. "What? Who?" I asked, as I looked away from the fireworks lighting the sky that Fourth of July. My wife was on the phone and began to tell me that one of the young boys in our church, who was about two years of age, had been playing in his bedroom and fell out of his window. He fell twelve feet down onto the concrete driveway. We immediately began to pray and made the necessary phone calls to deal with the situation.

While on the phone with one of my on-call associate pastors, I asked about the child's condition. "He is in the emergency room and is going through a series of tests, but we don't know anything more than that," was his reply.

Immediately I joined hands with my family and contacted other members in the church for prayer. We stood in our driveway and prayed, declaring that there not be one broken bone or any form of permanent damage. We established ongoing prayer in the church.

I remember backing out of my driveway as neighborhood fireworks lit up the sky around me. I prayed to the Lord, thinking about how He helped our great nation win its independence. I said, "Lord, it's the Fourth of July; deliver this child the way you delivered America. Intervene and do a miracle, I pray." I spoke the Word and prayed loudly in the spirit as I drove to the hospital.

I'll never forget the scene as I walked into the emergency room. There, on his back, lay one of the children from my church, strapped down, with a neck brace on him, in preparation for an MRI. When I was greeted by his mother, I remember her first words to me. She said, "Pastor, God is going to do a miracle, and all is well." I told her that I agreed and that there would not be any broken bones either.

We waited through test after test. We continued to pray and to speak God's Word until finally some news came. The doctor told us the boy was lucky to be alive. He said it was amazing that there were no internal injuries or broken bones. He only had a slight concussion. Thank God for His angelic protection and for a family and a church that didn't leave God alone until we obtained a miracle.

It is of vital importance to remember that our first words and initial reactions on hearing the news of a potential crisis can determine the outcome.

You never saw Jesus react in fear to bad news. During the storm in Mark 4:35–39, He slept. And when He was awakened by the disciples, His first words were, "Peace, be still" (verse 39). You didn't see Jesus wake up in a panic and tell everyone to hit the deck because of the raging wind.

On another occasion, when Lazarus was sick and about to die (John 11:1–12), notice that Jesus didn't react negatively to the news. He just spoke right and responded calmly. In fact, after hearing about Lazarus, He even stayed two days longer where He had been before heading over to see him.

Choosing the right first words is not only the most important response but also the most challenging. We have the power in our mouths to change situations and wreak havoc on the devil if we speak correctly. Proverbs 18:21 says, "Death and life are in the power of the tongue." Did you notice it said death first and then life? This is because people tend to gravitate first toward the negative when they are faced with difficulties.

A lifestyle of close fellowship with the Lord and meditating on His Word will help you respond correctly to the trials of life that arise. The right response will place you on the right road to victory.

REFUSE TO LOSE YOUR *LEVELS* OF AUTHORITY

I can say after pastoring Lord of Hosts Church from its start—more than ten years—that we have overcome many battles and have seen many victories. We have walked through numerous challenges that sometimes have felt similar to the ones experienced in Hebrews 11:32–33, which says:

And what shall I more say? for the time would fail me to tell of Gedeon, and of Barak, and of Samson, and of Jephthae; of David also, and Samuel, and of the prophets: Who through faith subdued kingdoms, wrought righteousness, obtained promises, stopped the mouths of lions.

The Lord wants us to experience the same victories the way they did in these verses. I have discovered a key to enjoying that victory comes through a determined pursuit of God and using the authority He gives us. In Hebrews 11:33, they were persistent to use four different *levels* of authority. They used the same methods God gave Adam clear back in Genesis 1:28. The Lord told him to *be fruitful, multiply, replenish,* and *subdue* the earth. These were the four levels of Adam's God-given authority. They are the same things reflected in Hebrews 11:33.

They have to do with taking what belongs to you through the kind of determined faith that will not take no for an answer. These heroes of faith in Hebrews received miracles because they were persistent to keep what was rightfully theirs. Not leaving God alone means that you don't give up your position easily or allow the devil to steal your goods the way Adam did. These four levels of authority also belong to us.

Four levels of authority

1. *Subdue kingdoms.* This was both in the natural and spiritual realms. This term meant "to conquer; bring into subjection or control." This was how Adam was supposed to subdue the earth. He was to be the owner of all the possessions God had given him, not hand them over to the devil. We also have the power and responsibility to keep what God has given us.

2. *Wrought righteousness.* In the Greek, these words mean "integrity, purity of life, correctness of thinking and acting." Adam was placed in the garden to reflect the righteousness of God. Like Adam, we are to replenish the earth by pouring righteousness back into it and enjoying the blessing that comes from a righteous lifestyle.

3. *Obtained promises.* This meant that they *obtained, attained,* and *received* the promises of God. They didn't just maintain what they already had, but they received new things from God. It was the way Adam was called to multiply and be fruitful. It wasn't enough to just keep what God had already given him. God wanted multiplication and productivity, and He does not want us to just maintain either. The Lord wants us to be productive and fruit bearing.

4. *Stop the mouths of lions.* They silenced and blocked the mouths of lions and the evil forces that sought to destroy them. This meant they had the power and authority *to tread, to reign, to rule over, and to govern a territory.* They were able to stand against any evil that was trying to steal from them without fear or intimidation. Adam had the right to war against Satan and tell him to leave. You can stop the devil's lies and attacks the same way.

So the four levels of authority are summed up as:

1. Keep what God gave you.
2. Live right.
3. Be productive for God.
4. Resist the devil.

For us to accomplish all that God wants—as He wanted from Adam—we must be determined to use these four levels of authority. We need to take what is rightfully ours and not give up. Decide you will not quit. Becoming a person who refuses to leave God alone means you are persistent to hold your ground and go forward. It means you won't be thrown off course until the end of the battle.

I thank God that through all the trials and experiences we have had to face together as a church family, we have remained determined not to leave God alone. Commitment to prayer keeps you determined, and it is the outlet to use your levels of authority. It will open the way to blessing like nothing else. If the prayer of one man, Moses, can release the entire nation of Israel—which was about to be gone in a few seconds—what can it do for our lives and cities?

This is what happened when the boy in the church fell from the window. Because of a commitment to prayer, our church was able to stand its ground at a moment's notice and take back what the devil wanted to steal from our hands. I teach my church how to pray corporately and individually, so they are quick to use their God-given authority. We are dedicated to seeking the Lord faithfully and not allowing prayer to lose its place of importance in our church. Without prayer, you will begin to compromise and let go of your possessions the way Adam did.

REFUSE TO LOSE YOUR *REALMS* OF AUTHORITY

Not only do you have authority on four levels, but also God has given you authority in four different *realms* as well. As I said, using your levels of authority means you are holding what rightfully belongs to you. Your four realms of authority, however, are the places God wants you to influence or govern. Let me explain this from Genesis 1:26, where it says, "And God said, Let us make man in our image, after our likeness: and let them have dominion over the fish of the sea, and over the fowl of the air, and over the cattle, and over all the earth, and over every creeping thing that creepeth upon the earth."

God wanted man to deal with four different realms that existed around him on the earth. He was designed by God with the internal ability to live seated above each of them. God created man to rule. That is why human beings are dominant over trees and animals and can govern all the earth's affairs.

Four realms of authority

1. *Fish of the sea.* This is authority to deal with things in the deep that we cannot see. God gives the believer power over all of the unseen demonic realm.

2. *Fowl of the air.* This is the authority we have over the high places of the enemy in the heavenlies. When God was creating the heavens and the earth in Genesis, there was only one thing He didn't call good—the firmament. This was because Lucifer, the devil, dwelt in the heavenlies and is called the prince of the power of the air (Ephesians 2:2).

3. *Cattle and all the earth.* The cattle and the earth both speak of the physical realm that we visibly see. Therefore we can deal in the governments, commerce, kingdoms, and territories where we live. Authority in the physical realm also represents the beastly nature of our natural flesh that we must take authority over.

4. *Every creeping thing.* I believe the creeping things are those things that try to crawl around and creep up on you in life. They speak of deceptive tactics and pitfalls. Let's face it; I don't like things that creep anyhow. I want to

step on them. Any subtle movement by the devil is under our feet.

With your four levels of authority, you must govern as a king and priest unto God (Revelation 1:6). You are His ambassador and representative sent to govern in all four realms. They are your sphere of influence given by God. You have the right to address them by speaking and to be involved with them both spiritually and physically. Standing in your realms of authority means you have the right to stand in bold faith and action in your nation. It also means that you can govern your mind against every deception. It further means you don't have to be intimidated to be all that God has called you to become. It means every place God sends you, you must submit to His authority on your life. If you are persistent, you will begin to see yourself stand confidently in every realm.

God wants His people to rise to the occasion and stand out as a voice. His examples in the Bible were determined to place their finger on all of the realms of our authority, and they refused to be silenced. Very simply, the four realms of authority you have the right to influence are:

1. Unseen realm
2. High places or heavenlies
3. Physical realm
4. Subtle places of deception

I AM LOCKING THE DOORS OF YOUR CHURCH

"I am locking the doors of your church, Hank, and you will not be allowed to meet here this Sunday or ever again." When I heard that, I was immediately gripped by fear.

"What? You can't be serious," I said, as I questioned the property manager of our church building at that time. He was stating that he was locking the doors of the church because we were not complying with tenant rules. We had an ongoing battle with the property manager and tenants next to us since we were meeting in a small, rented storefront bay.

When we signed our lease to hold services, we were just starting as a church. I had told the owners that the service would include praise and worship with instruments involving drums and guitars. The property manager at that time said it would be no problem. But no one had accounted for how thin the walls were between us and the other tenant. The neighboring tenant was an office setting that conducted seasonal business on weekends.

As you can imagine, it was very noisy for them on Sundays when we were having church. They were not too happy and reported the problem to the manager of the property. So the manager decided that we would have to move immediately, meaning they would not let us hold service on Sunday. They were going to lock the doors.

We had just a few days to figure out what to do since Sunday was fast approaching and we now needed a new place to meet. I called the few members of my newly formed church and told them what was happening. We prayed and asked the Lord for His direction, refusing to give up until God intervened.

Do you know what happened? A well-respected business professional—someone I didn't even know and who had never attended my church—caught wind of what was happening and came to our aid at the last minute. This person negotiated with the parties involved, and while we didn't know it at the time, God had a miracle in the making.

So the manager told us that, even though he could not let us keep the space, he was now willing to give us another space on a different part of the strip mall. The problem was, it was larger and more expensive. But we simply had no choice. We didn't know it at the time, but God was expanding our vision. We stepped out on the faith of our persistent prayers. The result was that we went from one small bay to three bays. Eventually we progressed until we gained seven times the space of that original small bay.

God miraculously used that situation to expand and bless us. We might have missed the blessing, however, if we had resorted to fear. Because a church refused to leave God alone, He powerfully took what the devil meant for evil and brought the church into blessing.

ACTS 12: THE CHURCH THAT DIDN'T LEAVE GOD ALONE

In Acts 12, we read about the early church that, through prayer, didn't let go of God. Again, prayer is what made the churches of the Book of Acts so powerful. They had the results and power that many churches don't see today. Why? Because they were diligent and knew how to get God's attention.

In Acts 12:1–3 we read, "Now about that time Herod the king stretched forth his hands to vex certain of the church. And he killed James the brother of John with the sword. And because he saw it pleased the Jews, he proceeded further to take Peter also." Not only was James killed, but now Peter was taken prisoner and about to lose his life too.

What did the church decide to do? They got smart and realized that one apostle was already gone and another was about to follow. The Bible didn't say they marched seven times around the jail cell with picket signs. They didn't bring a gift to Herod and try to convince him to free Peter. They didn't resort to the natural solution.

This is what a lot of Christians do. They go to some other method instead of refusing to leave God alone in prayer. But this church in Acts 12 went to persistent prayer. Acts 12:5 says, "Peter therefore was kept in prison: but prayer was made without ceasing of the church unto God for him." They refused to quit and give up. They made a decision to pray until Peter was released. And, of course, as the story goes, Peter got released because of their prayers. When he arrived at the house where they were praying, they thought he was a ghost. Can you imagine the surprise?

Sometimes when you pray, you don't always see the answer on the way while the trial is on you. You have to be careful to recognize the answer when it arrives on your doorstep. Often you just don't expect an answer because you don't understand that when we refuse to leave God alone, something powerful is going to take place.

When I was in high school, during gym class the teacher had us learn archery with real bows and arrows (or as real as they can be for high school). We would all stand in line and try to hit the target—especially the bull's-eye. Well, I had no experience shooting a bow and arrow, so I just shot recklessly without really thinking that I would actually hit the target, least of all the bull's-eye.

I had already assumed I wouldn't be a successful archer, so I shot aimlessly without any real determination. I spent most of the time goofing off. Archery is a sport that requires practice and commitment, so I didn't really try. My heart wasn't in it, so I lost interest quickly.

A flock of geese flew overhead, and I decided to shoot arrows into the air to be funny. The problem was that while shooting in the air, I didn't realize that my aimless arrows were landing on the other side of the hill where another gym class was running on the track. Needless to say, the archery class came to an abrupt end, with me in a lot of trouble. I realize today that by shooting at nothing, I came close to hitting the wrong target.

It's the same way with prayer. When people are halfhearted and aim at nothing, they end up with results they wish they didn't have. Either they don't pray at all or they pray in desperation, hoping something will work out. James 4:2–3 says, "Yet ye have not, because ye ask not. Ye ask, and receive not, because ye ask amiss." Believe you are able to accomplish your goal in prayer no matter how difficult it seems, and refuse to quit.

Jesus gave us a powerful principle for targeted prayer. In Matthew 7:7–8 He said, "Ask, and it shall be given you; seek, and ye shall find; knock, and it shall be opened unto you: For every one that asketh receiveth; and he that seeketh findeth; and to him that knocketh it shall be opened." He also said, "And whatsoever ye shall ask in my name, that will I do, that the Father may be glorified in the Son. If ye shall ask any thing in my name, I will do it" (John 14:13–14). These scriptures give us a picture of targeted prayer. We can see that it is not just firing out desperate prayers, hoping to get God's attention. It is aiming for a specific request and believing you're going to get a bull's-eye answer. It is prayer that refuses to give up until the desired answer is received—even when it appears things are not working out.

It is helpful to make a list of what you are praying about. Then go to the Bible to find a scriptural promise about your needs on the list, and worship the Lord over them. This will make your prayers become like prepared arrows. Armed this way, you can expect to receive an answer. Then it is important to put your hand on those written prayer requests every day and thank God for the bull's-eye.

One time I had a list of things I was praying. Not long after I prayed, I put the list away in a box and forgot about it. Years later, I came across that box with the list of requests in it. When I read over the list, I was shocked. I realized God was faithful to answer every one of those needs during a very difficult time in my life. I also realized that I had never thanked the Lord for them simply because I had forgotten about them. Now I am careful to thank the Lord for His faithful answers to my prayers.

THE CRY OF REFUSAL

Every one of us may have times when we need to cry out to God. James 5:4 says, "For listen! Hear the cries of the field workers whom you have cheated of their pay. The wages you held back cry out against you. The cries of those who harvest your fields have reached the ears of the Lord of Heaven's Armies" (NLT). In this verse, God heard the cry of people who were oppressed. Like them, we may have felt all alone or defrauded sometimes, but don't forget that the Lord is listening.

Even though He hears, however, God is not moved just because we yell, scream, or cry. This may make us feel better, but screaming is not the thing that will move God or change our circumstances. It is not the sound of our cry that the Lord looks for; it is the cry of faith and determination. This moves Him. It is how we cause Him to move so we can see results.

So in the previous scripture, He heard the cry of the oppressed. But let's see what kind of sound moves Him to act. Hebrews 11:6 says, "But without faith it is impossible to please him: for he that cometh to God must believe that he is, and that he is a rewarder of them that diligently seek him."

Even though God's ears may hear the cry of your oppression, He looks for more than the empty sound of crying. He is looking for a cry filled with a refusal to go away empty. This verse gives us three ingredients that—if He is going to move on your behalf—God looks for in your cry.

1. *Without faith it is impossible.* Believe God will always do what He says.

2. *Believe that He is.* Believe what the Bible says about Him.

53

3. *He is a rewarder of them who diligently seek Him.* Trust that He will reward those who refuse to quit and won't leave Him alone.

God wants you to cry out to Him in your situation because His ears are always open to the cry of the righteous. There is a note, however, that God looks for in every cry. There is a certain sound He wants to hear. It is not the cry of desperation. It is a cry of refusal, a refusal to leave God alone until you see His promises come to pass.

THOSE WHO REFUSED TO LEAVE GOD ALONE

The Bible is full of examples of those who refused to leave God alone. These people were not fictitious, nor were their stories fables. We must remember that the stories in the Bible actually happened. The people were not any different from us.

What kind of man was Elijah? Look at James 5:17, which says, "Elijah was a man just like us. He prayed earnestly that it would not rain, and it did not rain on the land for three and a half years" (NIV). Elijah was a normal human being just like you and me. If he could cause something miraculous to happen through persistent prayer, so can you. Here is a list of people in the Bible who simply refused to leave God alone. There may be more of them than you realized. From their examples, we can be encouraged that if they could do miracles by refusing to give up, then we can too.

- *Jacob:* He would not leave God alone until the Lord blessed him, and he became the nation of Israel (Genesis 32:26).

- *Moses:* When God wanted to be left alone, Moses refused and saved a nation (Exodus 32:10–14).

- *Hezekiah:* This king was destined to die, but he put his face to the wall in prayer. He refused to quit until he heard from God. Fifteen years were added to his life (2 Kings 20:1–6).

- *The church of Acts:* When this church was persecuted, great miracles took place because the people prayed and refused to leave God alone (Acts 4:31; Acts 12).

- *The Syrophoenician woman:* Having a daughter in need of a miracle, she refused to take no for an answer. Even after an apparent insult from Jesus, she still refused to leave Him alone, and she received healing for her daughter (Mark 7:25–30).

- *Blind Bartimaeus:* He refused to leave Jesus alone even when ignored, while others tried to prevent him. His determination caused him to receive his sight (Mark 10:46–54).

WHEN JESUS WANTED TO BE ALONE

Jesus went to a quiet place to be alone. It probably started as an ordinary day just like the others when the news came to Him, as it says in Matthew 14. It was the news that Jesus's cousin, John the Baptist, had just been beheaded. The Lord was visibly bothered by this because His cousin had been the forerunner of His ministry, the one who declared, "Behold! The Lamb of God who takes away the sin of the world!" (John 1:29, NKJV). The very one who seemed to understand His purpose was now gone.

After hearing this, Jesus went away to be left alone. We find the story in Matthew 14:12–13: "Then his disciples came and took away [John the Baptist's] body and buried it, and went and told Jesus. When Jesus heard it,

He departed from there by boat to a deserted place by Himself. But when the multitudes heard it, they followed Him on foot from the cities" (NKJV). Notice Jesus didn't even receive the news until after His cousin was already buried. What a shock that would be to most people. When He heard, He did not react in a panic, but departed by ship into a deserted place to be alone. Like most people, He just wanted a moment away.

When the multitudes discovered where He was, however, they followed Him out into the wilderness. Here the Son of God Himself just wanted to be alone, but the people refused to let Him. When Jesus saw their determination, He didn't turn them away. The Bible says He saw the great multitude, was moved with compassion toward them, and healed the sick. Look at Matthew 14:14. It says, "And Jesus went forth, and saw a great multitude, and was moved with compassion toward them, and he healed their sick."

When the people refused to leave Jesus alone, what was the result? He blessed them. He didn't turn them away, even when His human side just needed a moment.

What will happen when you pursue Him the way these people did? He will respond to you. When something troubles or hurts you, pray about it—not until you feel better for the moment, but until you see the answer manifest. Even when Jesus had it on His mind to do one thing, the persistence of the people caused Him to change His mind. It reveals how much He really loves us and how He will respond to our pursuit of Him. Even when He did not want to be with anyone, He responded to a hungry people.

To realize how incredible this was, put yourself in Jesus's shoes. Like most of us, I can understand a little what it is like not wanting to be bothered sometimes. Have you ever had a time when you just want a moment alone? Especially today with cell phones, faxes, and e-mail. Everyone expects you to be available at all hours to answer calls no matter what you have going on. The busiest times always seem to occur right when you want a quiet moment.

That is probably how Jesus was feeling. He just wanted a quiet moment to gather His thoughts. But when He saw the persistence of this multitude, He couldn't ignore them. I think there was just something inside of Jesus that couldn't resist a hungry people. Their refusal to leave Him alone was enough for Him to change His mind at that moment.

The Bible gives us further insight into the persistence of these people. Perhaps it is what stood out to Jesus and caused Him to respond to their needs. We find it in the same passage of Matthew 14, in verses 13–15:

- *They heard.* They didn't doubt what they heard about Jesus. Instead, they believed it.

- *They followed Him.* They put action behind what they believed. They did something physically to support their faith.

- *They followed Him on foot.* They didn't use the easiest method to get there. They followed Him even when they risked exhaustion.

- *They followed Him all day until evening.* They forgot about the time and continued even though it was late.

I believe God is looking for the modern-day church to follow Him with the same persistence of this multitude. They didn't doubt what they heard of Jesus, and they did something about it—even though it meant they might get tired or face a challenge doing so. They might have been tempted to quit. Nevertheless, they went after Him and sacrificed their time in order to get the manifestation of their miracle.

When Jesus saw that level of determination, He couldn't ignore their refusal to leave Him alone. It caused Jesus to change His mind about His plans for the day. And that group received what they came for.

The Gondola Man

What we need to decide is how bad we want our answer. I had something funny happen that the Lord used to show me the power of refusal when you want something really bad.

I had taken my family to have dinner in downtown Omaha. It was a very hot summer evening but still a good night for a walk after dinner in order to make room for some ice cream. There is a fountain downtown that shoots about three hundred feet in the air and lights turn the water different colors. It sits in the middle of a small city lake, and you can purchase gondola rides around the fountain. We thought it sounded fun and decided to ride on one.

Seeing the spray of the cool water, I thought it would be adventurous to get close enough to feel the water falling on us. I told my family, "Hey, let's see how close we can encourage the driver to get near the fountain." So I asked him, "Is there any way that you can get this boat right underneath that fountain over there?"

He laughed and said, "No, that fountain shoots three hundred feet, and it could possibly sink this boat. Besides that," he said, "my boss won't like it." I looked at my wife, and she was giving me the look that says I better not keep pressing him. But how bad did I want it?

On the boat with us was a couple about twenty years of age who were on a special date. I am sure they didn't want to ride under that water, but I wanted to get the boat under that fountain. So I kept bringing it up to everyone in the boat, about how unforgettable it would be if we went near the fountain.

Eventually, after a while, quite a few agreed that it would be fun, until finally we all took a consensus about going under the fountain. Nobody spoke up to protest, even the couple on the date. The gondola man told me that I didn't understand the water pressure, but I insisted that he could still get safely close. Right? By then even he was tempted, so he kept inching closer to the water spray.

Do you know what happened? We got so close we finally couldn't avoid it. Everyone's eyes got bigger, and the nice couple on the date were looking at one another with fear. Before we knew it, the water was above our heads high in the air. "Yes, we're going in!" I yelled.

We got right next to the edge of the fountain, and suddenly gallons of water came pouring down over the gondola. We were drenched. The poor couple on their date were screaming. I was soaked; so was my wife. She was soaked in another way too—like sore and mad. I suppose a few people in the boat didn't share my sense of adventure.

After the ride, we had to walk through the downtown area back to the car. I tried to tell my wife not to worry, that we would be dry by the time we got there. Not true; we went sloshing right through the middle of downtown on a Friday night.

The point of this story is that I was persistent. I was hot and I wanted to cool off. I didn't take no for an answer. Of course, I probably should have been more considerate of the other people, but they didn't speak up. They were silent about it, and my persistence won out.

What would happen if we refused to leave God alone that way? Just as the gondola driver changed his mind, we might see God respond like that to our determination. Ask yourself, how bad do you want it? In the Bible, the Lord responded to those who refused to give up while the passive ones got overlooked. Refuse to leave God alone until your answer manifests.

Yes, there will be opposition, and sometimes you will be tired enough to give up, especially when it feels like you are hitting one brick wall after another. Realize that many before you have felt the same thing. But if you refuse to quit, God will respond to your determination.

Don't give up. Press through until you receive what you need from the Lord.

4

I Will Not Leave You Alone
Until You Bless Me

And he said, Let me go, for the day breaketh. And he said,
I will not let thee go, except thou bless me.

—Genesis 32:26

It was with determination that Jacob held on to what he wanted. He said, "I will not let you go, except you bless me." This is what Jacob said when he wrestled with a man in Genesis 32:26. This was to be a statement that would be repeated by many men and women of God. It is the honest heartbeat of most believers who don't want to leave God alone. They want to pursue God until they see His best in their lives.

Most committed Christians want to stay intimately connected with God every day and in every situation. Yet many find themselves caught by distractions and schedules that tempt them to let God out of their sight, even knowing they have still come short of His available blessing.

Jacob had to find the determination within himself to endure for the blessing and the answers he needed. This is what God the Father is looking for from us.

Typically, most people want to experience the blessings from God, but few are willing to fight past their present circumstances to receive what the Lord has promised them. Something occurred with Jacob, causing him to grab ahold of God until he got what he needed.

The Lord does not want you always coming up short of the answer. Like the old saying goes, "It's not how you start but how you finish." From Jacob's experience, we see him persist until he received, even when it seemed like his answer might be getting away from him. The devil wants it to appear as if God is a million miles away and not going to respond to you. But from Jacob's experience, we can also see that God was there. He was well within his reach. He was touchable to Jacob's situation. God is within your reach too, but He wants to know if you will press toward Him until your manifestation of blessing comes. The Lord is there if you will reach out to Him.

Jacob wrestled with a man who the Bible gives us clear indication was God Himself. Genesis 32:30 says, "Jacob named the place Peniel (which means 'face of God'), for he said, 'I have seen God face to face, yet my life has been spared'" (NLT). Whom did Jacob see? Jacob said he saw God face-to-face, and therefore he called the name of that place Peniel—a word that literally means "the face of God."

Some translations say he wrestled with an angel. But the entire account reveals that Jacob's experience was much more significant. It was very different from many of the other places in Scripture where people encountered angels.

This moment was a special one because God was creating a nation; He was remaking a man. Jacob was the man who was going to be a picture of the church—the spiritual Israel. Because of this, I believe he literally had to have an encounter with Christ, the Lord of the church. This is why he wrestled with such determination; he was experiencing a transformation process that left him feeling inadequate and in need of God's blessing. God was doing something supernatural with his character.

This is the example of the church and how God remolds us into the image of Christ. We know Jacob experienced a transformation because the Lord changed his name from Jacob, meaning "deceiver," to Israel, meaning "God rules" and "one who strives *with* God." The Lord was converting him from a habit of deception into a person of determined persistence who, in spite of his previous disappointments, became totally dependent on the Lord.

This is what God wants to do with you and me. He wants to transform us into stable people who believe the Lord's promises—no matter what happens. Many people are not persistent in the spirit because past disappointments keep them from seeing a powerful future. Like Jacob, they need an experience with the Lord that will transform them. They need an encounter with the face of God so they will never give up on their quest for His blessing, even when it seems easier to stop.

We must become people totally submitted to God and who are persistent to receive His best. This is why Jacob's encounter is so vital for us to see. In order to represent the future church, this man, Jacob, needed a divine encounter with Jesus Christ. Once that occurred, it did something that created determination in him to not leave the Lord alone until he was blessed.

The verse says God asked Jacob to let go because daytime was near. Notice he wrestled at night, which speaks of facing your darkest hour—the moment when you feel the most alone. Once again, it seemed that God was playing hard to get, and His promises were difficult to hold on to. We know, however, that was not the case.

Instead, God was looking for someone who would persist. He wanted someone who was determined for His blessing and willing to pay a price to experience it. So it is as if the Lord was making it appear as though He needed to leave, but all the while He was waiting for a reason to stay.

This seems to be a consistent thread to God's character in the Bible. We also find it in Luke 24:28–29, which says, "And they drew nigh unto the village, whither they went: and he made as though he would have gone further. But they constrained him, saying, Abide with us." It seemed as if Jesus was going to go on without them. Undoubtedly, it was to see what their response would be. Maybe Jesus just wanted to be invited to stay with them. They could have let Him go on, but they pressed Him to stay.

Often we do not realize that the Lord wants to be invited to stay, to be included in our business. God wants you to be the one who initiates including Him and showing that you cannot live without Him. He has already shown us that by sending Jesus. He is our example. Look again at Luke 24:29, "They begged him, 'Stay with us!'" (CEV).

He wants us to reciprocate that expression in our actions every day. Of all the things we can learn about our relationship to the Lord, He wants to see if we will still follow Him, even when it seems He isn't moving as we expect Him to. He wants us to pursue Him and His promises in an unconditional way.

Are we determined? We have to ask ourselves if we are determined to pursue Him even when our breakthrough seems to be miles away, even when it seems God is not there. Will we grab ahold of Him until we see His blessings? Will we invite Him to stay with us?

FOREVER MARKED BY HIM

After Jacob had this powerful experience with God, not only was he changed, but he was also forever marked as a result of it. Genesis 32:25, 31–32 says, "When the man saw that he could not win, he struck Jacob on the hip and threw it out of joint.... The sun was coming up as Jacob was leaving Peniel. He was limping because he had been struck on the hip, and the muscle on his hip joint had been injured. That's why even today the people of Israel don't eat the hip muscle of any animal" (CEV).

Jacob fought until the man finally had to put his thigh out of joint. That must have been very painful—a moment I am sure he never forgot. Now Jacob's fight began as a struggle to fight for the rights of his own flesh, but something happened that changed his fight from fighting for his own rights to fighting for God's blessing. There is a difference.

When his thigh was taken out of joint, it was a life-changing experience. His thigh represented his own strength to stand. He needed to know that depending on God's blessing for your life is always better than your power to stand on your own. Once you have a life-changing experience with God, you are forever marked—forever changed. Your walk will be different.

If you are forever changed by the Lord, your life will bear the fruit of it, a permanent mark, as Jacob's did. There will be a spiritual "limp" that says you have cut away your own rights.

God does not use harm or tragedy to cause that to happen in your life. Jacob's physical example was the picture of what God wants you to submit to spiritually. God wants you marked by His power in such a way that you show that your flesh is no longer in control.

The story in Genesis 32 tells us there was a moment when Jacob seemed to prevail during the fight, until his thigh was taken out of joint. It was not that Jacob literally prevailed physically against the power of the Lord, but he was prevailing in his own fleshly will and determination. He fought to retain his own fleshly independence. He had to learn reliance on the power of God instead of the means of deception he was previously accustomed to using. Jacob had to be emptied of himself and determined to trust in the power of the Lord until the fruit or blessing of it manifested in his life.

It is said, historically, that Jacob walked with a limp for the rest of his life. For him, this was a perpetual reminder of how futile natural abilities are. He finally realized that he could not rely on his own strength to devise his way through life. He literally felt it when he didn't "have a leg to stand on."

People who have had a face-to-face encounter with God will always *walk* differently from those who have not. Jacob's limp marked him as a man who was transformed into someone who would never leave the Lord alone. From a beginning as a deceiver to being referenced as a prince who carried the power of God, his wrestling match is a picture of a true conversion. Every man is forever marked after he comes in contact with God this way, and God wants all of us to have that experience. Jacob was commended because he was willing to endure that conversion process until he couldn't live without His blessing. It was that experience that gave him confidence to expect God to bless him. That mark on his life was visible to all.

People will notice that there is something different about you when you are marked with God's favor because you were persistent to stay with Him. There is nothing better than having a life marked with the blessings of God.

Once when I was in prayer, I decided to have a special time of just worship and thanksgiving. I told the Lord I wasn't there to make any requests or ask Him for anything; I just wanted to *hang out*. Then I felt the Lord tell me that He appreciated how I just wanted to be with Him—without asking for anything. Of course God wants to bless us. But there comes a time when we need to be concerned with what is on the heart of the Father and what *He* is interested in talking about.

Do you know that even though I was just trying to bless the Lord, I still felt Him trying to give back to me? I said, "Lord, this is about You today." I was surprised the Lord didn't give up on it easily. I kept feeling that nudge of the Spirit that wanted me to ask Him for something. The more He persisted, the more I tried to say that I just wanted to praise Him. I felt myself wrestle back and forth with the Lord. I really didn't want to ask Him for anything, but do you know He just seemed determined to bless me? Of course, I caved in. He marked me for His blessing, praise God! And everything I prayed for that day I received.

I learned something from that time of prayer. My motive was to bless the Lord, and His motive was to not let *me go* until He blessed me instead. I want to encourage you to reach out today and not let go of the Lord. Be persistent with Him about everything that concerns you. You will find your life marked with His favor and blessing.

WHEN YOU WRESTLE TO GET YOUR ANSWER

Have you ever struggled to receive your much-needed answers from God? Learning to walk in the blessing of God is a lifelong process that requires discipline and faithfulness. Like Jacob, we may find ourselves wrestling for it sometimes.

We will wrestle many things to live in the blessing of God. Not only will we wrestle with God to let go of our own fleshly desires, but we will also wrestle in the fight of faith to remain determined to walk in all the promises of God—even when the devil is trying to discourage us. This is why Jacob's experience with God is an example for you and me.

Naturally speaking, wrestling is a sport that takes stamina, strength, speed, and skill. Unlike boxing, it is rarely over in seconds. Wrestling can go on for quite some time until one of the opponents is totally exhausted and gives up. All of us are wrestlers engaged in a match that lasts all our lives.

When I was in junior high and decided to try out for the wrestling team, I was a skinny little kid with absolutely no muscle or meat on me. I wrestled at about 89 pounds and knew nothing about wrestling except what I saw on television.

There I was in my first year of wrestling, ready to face off with my opponent. I started off bent over with my hands touching the mat. The whistle blew, and I was on my back instantly as the referee was slapping the mat counting one, two, three. I was shocked! I realized that I had been pinned as soon as the match started. My opponent pushed my head, knocked me to the ground, and pinned me. Within a total of four seconds it was all over. Four seconds! It was probably a state record. How embarrassing.

Perhaps that is how your life feels—flat on your back and down for the count. We must understand that walking with God and receiving His continual blessings is a lifelong process. Don't give up too easily. Learn to press in until you receive what you need from the Lord. It isn't that He is keeping it from you, but He wants you to learn the art of stamina and strength in the spirit—so the devil cannot take you out in only four seconds.

I remember many times of fighting for God's blessings in my life, and God had to teach me the art of spiritual endurance and faith. Early in our marriage, my wife and I struggled while learning to obey God financially. We counted every penny trying to make ends meet. We wrestled and used our faith every way we knew how. We tithed and gave offerings; we held on to the Word of the Lord and His promises of prosperity. It was a "process," and we had to wrestle to receive God's blessings.

Our particular habit at the grocery store was to carry a calculator so we wouldn't spend beyond the few dollars we had available. The word *money* felt like such a depressing word then. Finally, one day I broke with the Lord. Determined that I had been shackled to the "process" long enough, I went to the grocery store without the little calculator—it almost felt like heresy. I wasn't trying to spend foolishly, but we needed a breakthrough, and I had to come to a place where I was going to rely on faith or die.

I remember sweating as every grocery item went across the checkout counter. God was watching our determination to trust Him and our ability to walk out the fight of faith. He was seeing if we were going to fight for His blessing or simply give up.

During those years, we also needed God's blessing for our cars. Not only did the car blessing seem as though it was a million miles away, but it also wasn't something we had the faith to even wrestle for. Every car we had was bad. We owned several different cars, some of which had been obtained from friends or family members. They were rusted-out cans of nothing—except one that was in average condition, but it was so big it seemed like you could land a plane on the hood.

One car especially was so bad that it created a fire anytime it idled beyond about three minutes. We didn't know this when we bought it for four hundred *borrowed* dollars until one snowy morning when I started it to let it warm up while I went back in the house to finish getting ready for work. Randomly glancing out the window, I saw flames under the hood.

"The car is on fire!" I screamed, and ran from the house into the driveway. All the while I kept yelling, "The car is on fire! The car is on fire!" And I frantically ran around looking for a way to put it out because, from all the movies I ever saw, a car on fire was a bad thing.

I couldn't seem to think clearly, but I knew I shouldn't raise the hood. So I grabbed some snow from the ground and wildly threw it all over the hood and on the grille where I could see the flames. After a frenzy of snow-throwing in the driveway, I somehow managed to douse the blaze. But I probably should have let the thing keep burning. Not only did our many bad cars serve as an embarrassment, but they also made it seem like God wasn't always paying attention to our struggles. Even when I wanted to feel angry and kick the tires sometimes, we managed to stay determined in our faith that God was eventually going to bless us.

We were tirelessly committed to practice every Bible principle we knew. We sowed seed, we gave, and we spoke the Word. For years we wrestled—we were not going to let God get away until He blessed us.

Then one day it came.

I had just returned home from a ministry trip when the phone rang. The person on the other line was being very persistent, saying he wanted to come and visit me. Now, I really didn't want any company because I had just arrived home and I was tired. I tried to tell the person on the phone that I had just arrived back from preaching out of town, but he didn't want to take no for an answer. He said, "Hank, you really need to let me come see you because I have something important to give you."

So I gave in, and about two hours later, he came over. We visited in the house awhile, and then this person asked me to come outside to the car. Then to my absolute shock, he handed me the car keys and said, "It's yours."

My wife and I were speechless. It was a brand-new luxury car, and this person told us that we could either drive it or trade it in for something else we wanted.

Do you know what? For a moment, I couldn't believe what was happening to the point that I almost tried to say no. My mind was filled with all kinds of crazy thoughts like: "I don't deserve this." "What will other people think?"

The devil *wants* to prevent you from receiving from the Lord. He *wants* you to give up early because, if you live without God's blessing long enough, you will start to see yourself as unworthy to receive anything good in your life. You develop a mental picture of yourself always doing without—then he wins because he has made you doubt God's promises. That's why it's so important not to quit until you receive *everything* that has been promised to you.

Just simply do not let go—no matter how long it seems to take you. God's blessing will manifest in your life if you wrestle for it without giving up.

THE SEED PROCESS WILL GROW YOUR BLESSING

One of the first ways to come into blessings is to understand seed, time, and harvest. This is why the Bible says as long as this earth remains, there will be seed, then time, which results into a harvest of blessings: "While the earth remaineth, seedtime and harvest, and cold and heat, and summer and winter, and day and night shall not cease" (Genesis 8:22).

When it comes to God's blessings, we usually want them instantly. Especially in a microwave society, we want everything now. Many people don't want the wrestling or the process it takes to receive the blessings of God. As we can see from this verse in Genesis, it starts first with a seed, then there is a seedtime—the time it takes for the seed to grow—and after that the result is a harvest of blessing.

Just as physical seeds need a period of time for them to germinate and grow, so do our spiritual seeds. During that period of growth, we have to care for the seeds and water them. It takes a commitment and sometimes a lot of patience. This is where many people miss out on enjoying the fullness of God's promises and blessings. They don't want a lifelong process or a growing season. They are impatient in waiting for the seed to mature and bear fruit, so they quit early.

When God created the earth, He intended for it to be a blessing. He wanted everything to grow and produce something good. Everything was created with seed-reproducing ability—the ability to produce after its own kind. In other words, He didn't *just* make a tree. God gave trees the ability to give forth seed that would produce more trees.

He did the same when He created man. He also gave man the ability to give forth seed that would produce children. Genesis 1:11–12 says, "And God said, Let the earth bring forth grass, the herb yielding seed, and the fruit tree yielding fruit after his kind, whose seed is in itself, upon the earth: and it was so. And the earth brought forth grass, and herb yielding seed after his kind, and the tree yielding fruit, whose seed was in itself, after his kind: and God saw that it was good."

When you realize that everything in the earth revolves around a seed process, you will not find it as difficult to endure with God and to trust Him for His promises. You can just wait through the growing season until the harvest comes. Yes, there will be times when it will feel hot and dry, and it may seem like every possible pestilence is trying to trample your garden.

There will be times when you don't feel like watering your garden because wrestling against the elements will get the better of you. But stay strong. The fight for your harvest is far less painful than what could happen if you didn't plant any seeds at all. You had nothing *before* you planted the seeds, so you are certainly better off fighting for them now.

In other words, don't quit wrestling, don't stop sowing toward your goal, and most of all, don't give up on God's promises. Don't stop believing. Those results—the fulfillment of the promises that God gave you—are your harvest.

When I was in elementary school, I had my first lesson in the principle of planting a seed and the time it takes to produce the plant. We had a class experiment where we all planted seeds in a Styrofoam cup full of dirt. The teacher taught us how to give it sunlight and water. I remember how it seemed to take a long time for those seeds to do anything. So when curiosity got the better of me, I dug into the dirt to check. There was no change—nothing!

Days later, every cup was growing something except for mine. When the teacher asked me about my plant, I told her that I had been digging in the dirt to check it. Well, as you know, that was why it never grew. I was disturbing the process by constantly checking on it.

Isn't this exactly what we do when it comes to receiving blessings from God? We become impatient with the process, and we tend to check the status of it on our own. We try to help God grow it. But what we don't always realize is, by doing that, we are only interrupting the process of growth that will manifest our answers.

Jesus reiterated this process of seed, time, and then harvest in Mark 4:26–29, when He said, "God's kingdom is like seed thrown on a field by a man who then goes to bed and forgets about it. The seed sprouts and grows—he has no idea how it happens. The earth does it all without his help: first a green stem of grass, then a bud, then the ripened grain. When the grain is fully formed, he reaps—harvest time!" (THE MESSAGE).

Sowing seeds toward your harvest can be summed up in one simple way: pursue God by making His kingdom your priority. That means you give of yourself to Him in every way you are able. Seed sowing is found in a lifestyle that is totally sold out to God and His kingdom. Sometimes your seeds will be financial offerings, and other times the seeds will be your time that is given—whether serving within the body of Christ or just spending time privately in prayer.

Once you have sown seeds toward your blessing, the key is to keep those seeds watered while you wait out the "seedtime" period. Watering means you don't throw your hands in the air halfway through and quit when you are in a spiritual drought. Basically, you can water it by praising God and talking about His promises. Speak about your answer that is on the way. Then rejoice and wait patiently until the harvest, because it will come.

Jesus used one very powerful word in Mark 4. It is the word that we all want to hear, and it's the pinnacle of His lesson. The word is *reap*. So if your goal is to reap, it means you stay in the "gardening business" until it is time to *harvest* the fruit from it.

Some harvests have longer growing seasons than others do, so waiting through the time element requires patience. You may not always know how long that growing season will be—especially if you have not planted that type of seed or reaped that kind of harvest before. But there is no other way to enjoy the harvest of blessing God has for you. Whether it is a need for healing, finances, or some other type of harvest you want to receive, don't quit until you are blessed. And don't quit until you receive the desired result of reaping your harvest.

Remember, every harvest starts with seeds. When we think of seeds, our focus usually turns to finances. That's normal because I have found that there are two primary problem areas everyone will deal with at some point or another in their life. These two things will be something you will need to pray about and need a harvest of God's blessing to deal with. Those two things are *healing* and *finances.*

Of all the things people struggle through, and all that people seem to deal with before they die, these two are the most dominant. More people die sick and broke than anything else. This is why God tells us in His Word, "Beloved, I wish above all things that thou mayest prosper and be in health, even as thy soul prospereth" (3 John 2).

I can't understand why some people will debate that God even wants to help us in these two areas, especially when healing and finances are the two main issues people face—daily. With finances in particular, some say money is evil and to stay away from it. But if you think about it, you can't even turn on a light switch without money!

I have never heard about money committing any crimes. Instead, it's people with the wrong heart who commit crimes with money or because of money. Money in and of itself is not evil. Money is just paper and coins. Scripture says it is the *love of money* that is the root of all evil (1 Timothy 6:10). When you keep your heart right with God and work to make Him your first love and passion, you can have money and use it righteously.

In the right perspective, God wants us to enjoy life and have nice things. You have a right to it if you tithe and give offerings as the Bible teaches. We only run into trouble with the *love of money* when our hearts become self-indulgent in our focus and God is forgotten. God wants you to feel confident asking Him to meet your financial needs. He is not offended if you wrestle for His financial blessing. According to Scripture, God says:

> Command those who are rich in this present world not to be arrogant nor to put their hope in wealth, which is so uncertain, but to put their hope in God, who richly provides us with every-

thing for our enjoyment. Command them to do good, to be rich in good deeds, and to be generous and willing to share. In this way they will lay up treasure for themselves as a firm foundation for the coming age, so that they may take hold of the life that is truly life.

—1 Timothy 6:17–19, NIV

Using these verses of Scripture, let me show you five things that God says we can do with our money:

1. We must not be arrogant about it (verse 17).
2. We cannot put our trust in it (verse 17).
3. We can enjoy it (verse 17).
4. We must do good with it and use it for the right things (verse 18).
5. We must be generous and willingly give it (verse 18).

When you keep these attitudes and principles in perspective, you can ask for God's financial blessing with a pure heart. Go ahead and ask God, stand on His promises, and don't let go until your answer comes.

Some people still don't believe God wants them blessed, so they would never think about approaching Him in the same manner that Jacob did. But Jacob, of course, was not God's only example of persistence. The Bible is full of persistent people who didn't give up easily. When we see their examples, it makes it easier for you and me to realize that we are not alone in our quest to enjoy a life filled with God's favor and blessing.

Here are a few examples of people who wrestled and overcame many obstacles to experience something wonderful from the Lord.

- *Zacchaeus* climbed a sycamore tree and was persistent until he got a visit from Jesus. (See Luke 19:1–10.)

- *The woman with the issue of blood* was persistent to press through the crowd until she touched Jesus even when she was frail and sickly. (See Mark 5:25–34.)

- *The Syrophoenician woman* was persistent when requesting a healing for her daughter, even after Jesus seemed like He wasn't going to answer her request. (See Mark 7:24–30.)

- *The multitudes* were persistent to follow Jesus out of the cities and received healing and the provision of food, even though Jesus came to be alone after the death of John the Baptist. (See Matthew 14:13–22.)

I discovered something about determined persistence when I was a preteen and decided to try my hand at babysitting. My first babysitting job was for a single parent who had a son named Billy. When his mom would leave, he would hang on my leg anytime he wanted something. He had the strongest grip of any child I knew.

He was a real "Billy the Kid." I could not get him off me. I would be walking around his house, and even outside, with this little kid hanging on my leg and sitting on my foot everywhere I went. I would try everything to shake him off, but to no avail. He would just look up at me, stick out his tongue, and say, "I'm not letting go until you give me what I want."

He would always wear me down. I would give in and give him what he wanted just to have some peace. That's right, the whole bag of cookies or candy. I would give him whatever it took. If I didn't give in, he would hang on my leg all night and threaten to tell his mom that I mistreated him. This was my first job, and I didn't want to get fired. And this boy was very determined about what he wanted.

ARE YOU LOOKING FOR A "NET" OR "NETS" BLESSING?

When we devote our lives to God, we will enjoy life more when we do things the way God says. Otherwise we will end up frustrated and upset at unanswered prayers or unattained blessings.

Once when Peter had fished all night, the Bible says he had caught nothing. Luke 5:5 says he reported this to Jesus by saying, "Master, we have toiled all night and caught nothing" (NKJV).

Does this sound familiar? You work all day but never seem to get ahead? You pray and never seem to get an answer? Life can be challenging, and sometimes we don't get the results we want. But Jesus gave Peter the very thing he needed to enjoy blessing. The entire story says:

> When [Jesus] had stopped speaking, He said to Simon, "Launch out into the deep and let down your *nets* for a catch." But Simon answered and said to Him, "Master, we have toiled all night and caught nothing; nevertheless at Your word I will let down the *net*." And when they had done this, they caught a great number of fish, and their net was breaking. So they signaled to their partners in the other boat to come and help them. And they came and filled both the boats, so that they began to sink. When Simon Peter saw it, he fell down at Jesus' knees, saying, "Depart from me, for I am a sinful man, O Lord!" For he and all who were with him were astonished at the catch of fish which they had taken.
> —Luke 5:4–9, NKJV, emphasis added

Notice what Jesus asked Peter to do. He told Peter to let down his *nets*—plural. Peter responded by saying he would let down the *net*—singular. So Peter didn't fully obey what Jesus said.

How many times does Jesus tell us to give—or to obey Him in some other way—and we don't do exactly as He says? The account in Luke 5 tells us that Peter received a great multitude of fish. But what would have happened if he had let down *nets* instead of the *net*, as Jesus had said? Just imagine how much more blessing he could have received.

Out of tiredness and frustration from an unproductive night of fishing, Peter did the minimum of what was required to get a blessing from the Lord. This is how we respond to the Lord many times. We don't want to fight or wrestle, so we are satisfied with a partial blessing rather than an abundant one.

We don't have to settle for a partial blessing. We can receive the full benefit God has for us. Jacob didn't want a partial blessing either, but rather one that required work, determination, energy, and persistence in not leaving God alone until he was blessed. He was willing to persist, even when it was a challenge to do it.

It can be summed up like this: the greater the effort you make to reach toward God, the greater the reward of blessing you will receive. How much do you want to reach for Him? You must grab ahold of God and not let go until your life is full of all He wants for you!

5

I Will Not Leave You Alone
Until You Deliver Me

In God I will praise his word, in God I have put my trust;
I will not fear what flesh can do unto me.... When I cry
unto thee, then shall mine enemies turn back: this I know;
for God is for me.

—Psalm 56:4, 9

You can make demon powers run in terror. You can make the devil terrified of you by one simple action. These verses from Psalm 56 tell us that he hates it when you do one thing—when you cry with your voice to the Lord.

The last thing demons want to hear is your voice calling out to God in prayer. I can see the demons placing their hands over their ears and screaming, "No, not that! They are calling on the power of God!" It is this very thing that freezes them in their tracks and forces them to turn around.

No wonder Satan wants to distract you from praying. Prayer is a powerful weapon against him. Evil spirits will use all sorts of harassments to try to make you lose your prayer focus. But when you put your foot down—when you refuse to put up with the harassment—and call out to the Creator of the universe, God turns the devil upside down. He defeats your enemies. When you pray, you have no need to doubt that God is for you and that He is fighting on your behalf.

Choosing not to leave God alone is an essential part to your deliverance. There are many situations and things to be delivered from—not all of them are directly associated with evil spirits. There is, of course, actual deliverance from evil spirits or bondage, but also there is deliverance from hurtful or harmful situations. Not all of these situations have to do with demons directly. For example, you can be delivered from debt or marital strife, which may have less to do with demons and more to do with human choices. Still, we will see God's power in both.

Sometimes when you begin to cry out to God in prayer, it may seem like nothing is happening. For the children of Israel, it first looked like God was ignoring them. Israel had been in bondage for four hundred years when God delivered them from Egypt. Exodus 14 records that during their departure, Pharaoh pursued them, and, for a moment, it almost looked as though God wasn't going to do anything to help them. Pharaoh's chariots were getting closer. It probably looked as if there was no time left and it was too late.

Then in verse 15, "The Lord said to Moses, Wherefore criest thou unto me? speak unto the children of Israel, that they go forward." Once again God was trying to provoke a response of faith from Moses and the children of Israel so He could display His delivering power. It wasn't that He didn't want to hear the cry of Moses, because we know Moses was confident in the delivering power of God.

This is where many people are in life; they have "Pharaoh" after them, they undoubtedly believe in God's deliverance, but they don't *do* anything. Moses needed to *do* something—he needed to *act* on the power of God. Even when it looked like there was no hope left, deliverance came when someone stood in the authority of God's power.

SURROUNDED BY GANGS

A number of years ago, I saw God's delivering power work for me in a very supernatural way. I had to act on the power of God without any time to think about it. I received a revelation on the verse from Psalm 56:9 that says, "*This I know*; for God is for me!" (emphasis added).

At the time, I was a youth pastor, and we had a special overnighter for the boys on the church campus. Later that night we took the whole group outside to play capture the flag. It was incredible fun until I started to get an uneasy feeling that something wasn't right. I told the other youth leaders that we should end the game and head back inside right away.

One of the other leaders—an off-duty police officer—asked me what was wrong. I said I wasn't sure, but I knew the Holy Spirit was warning me about something. We started getting all the kids inside the buildings when we heard the sound of a heavy-bass beat from a car stereo.

A large group of cars suddenly came filing into the parking lot. Seeing the cars, I started to run and tell the others to hurry and get inside with the kids. Then I began to pray in the spirit. The noise became louder as the cars came closer to us. It seemed like there were about seventy-five cars—of course, everything looks bigger when you are afraid and it's dark.

We kept ushering the kids inside, and all of them made it indoors. The off-duty police officer had run to another area to get his badge and weapon. He had it with him because he was scheduled to go to work in just a few hours. I was running across the grounds to make certain everyone was inside when, before I realized what was happening, I was surrounded by a crowd of gang members. They were everywhere!

Then one of the gang members—I suspect it was one of the leaders—began to walk toward me. He was wearing a long coat, holding some kind of long object, and he said something in a foreign language.

I was frozen. I couldn't say anything. I wanted to, but nothing would come out of my mouth! Feeling that I should do something to try and save myself, I put a stern look on my face, glared at him, and thrust my arm up with my finger pointing toward his face—I still couldn't speak though.

They could have killed me right there! But when I pointed my finger at him, he looked at me and his eyes got big. He and the others began to back away in shock. To this day I have no idea what they saw or heard, but they all started frantically running away to their cars. I don't even know what made them run.

In an effort to get out of there in a hurry, they even had a few fender benders in the parking lot. It was amazing! By the time the off-duty police officer made it back, they were almost gone. We all could not believe what had just happened. But we knew God had delivered us from them.

I have always wondered for certain what made them run, but I am convinced that something happened when I pointed my finger at him. I remember doing it because I knew that I needed to act on something in the power of the Spirit. As afraid as I was at the time, the authority of God was on me when I did it. It was the only thing I knew to do at a moment's notice. I didn't feel very confident, but I stepped out anyhow.

Maybe Moses didn't feel very confident when he pointed his rod at the Red Sea. But when you stand before the Lord and act on His power, God will move to deliver you. It makes that scripture come alive: "THIS I KNOW; for God is for me!" You just have to *know* that God is for you and that He is there to deliver you.

I think the man and his gang friends not only encountered the delivering anointing, but I believe they also saw God's angels. Whenever God delivered the people in the Bible, angels were involved there too; the angel of the Lord, for example, put a pillar of fire between the chariots of Pharaoh and the children of Israel. (See Exodus 14:19–20.)

We need to have a regular awareness as people of persistent prayer—who don't leave God alone—that angels will be working around us all the time. Look at Psalm 34:7: "The angel of the LORD encamps around those who fear him, and he delivers them" (NIV). This verse says the Lord's angel is there for people who fear God. People who fear God are those who stay close to Him, pursue Him, and refuse to leave Him alone.

You should expect angels to be there for you when you need help. They are assigned to deliver you. In Hebrews 1:14, the Bible says God's angels are sent to minister for us—those who are the heirs of salvation.

So how well are we protected? Have you ever thought about how many angels there are? If our eyes were opened to the spirit realm, we could see that there are far more angels with us than there are demons against us. Second Kings 6:15–17 says, "And when the servant of the man of God was risen early, and gone forth, behold, an host compassed the city both with horses and chariots. And his servant said unto him, Alas, my master! how shall we do? And he answered, Fear not: for they that be with us are more than they that be with them. And Elisha prayed, and said, LORD, I pray thee, open his eyes, that he may see. And the LORD opened the eyes of the young man; and he saw: and, behold, the mountain was full of horses and chariots of fire round about Elisha."

The servant of Elisha saw that there was real potential for a fight on their hands and he was filled with terror, so the prophet prayed that the servant's eyes would be opened into the spirit. When the servant saw into the spirit, he found that there were many more angels on their side than the enemy soldiers had available. That is because one-third of the angels fell when Lucifer did, so there are still two-thirds of heaven's angels who are available to us. We have the majority!

Angels are working powerfully everywhere to deliver the righteous and those who are in pursuit of God. Scriptures compare them to the wind and also to fire. This is important in the power of deliverance because wind is everywhere. And fire represents the power of Pentecost.

Psalm 104:4 says, "He makes winds his messengers, flames of fire his servants" (NIV). And in Hebrews 1:7, "In speaking of the angels he says, 'He makes his angels winds, his servants flames of fire'" (NIV). Remember in Acts 2:1–4 both wind and fire came on Pentecost. Angels undoubtedly accompanied the Holy Ghost on the wind. So that means when the Holy Spirit came, He didn't come alone—praise God!

I believe we are about to see a renewed visitation of angels in the body of Christ. These are angels who are assigned for our deliverance!

THE VISIONS OF DELIVERING ANGELS

Once when I was ministering overseas, I called a man from the audience and began to prophesy to him. I told him by a word of knowledge that I knew he was a pastor and that an angel was standing behind him. The Lord then showed me another man—a government official—who was persecuting this man's ministry. What I didn't know was that this pastor had even been put in jail because of this persecution. I told this pastor that the Lord had sent this angel to deal with the situation, and it was all about to change.

The next day the hosting pastor told me that during the night, the government official who was behind all the persecution had died! Yes, all the persecution stopped after that. Glory to God for His delivering angels.

Things like this shouldn't be a surprise to us. In Acts 12:20–23, the Bible says Herod persecuted the church, and he also was struck by an angel and died.

On another occasion, I was praying in a church and saw a vision. I saw huge angels standing at the doors of the auditorium. They looked very serious, but they showed no emotion. They all had swords that were drawn and were pointing them toward the ground.

Suddenly the doors of the church opened. Evil beings wearing brown robes with hoods entered the auditorium, walking right past the angels with a mocking attitude. I remember thinking, "Why aren't those angels doing anything?"

The druidlike people began to laugh, dance down the aisles of the full auditorium, and mock those in attendance. They even laughed at the prayer room. When one of them pointed at the pulpit and mocked the preaching, I thought, "Lord, this is awful. How can this be happening?"

Again one of them spoke loudly and, in front of everyone, said, "I will divide this church in one year in many ways!" Then they laughed again and danced out of the church.

Afterward, the Lord let me know that because prayer in the church was lacking, the angels were able to do nothing to stop the event. Sometime later, that vision literally happened when people actually told the church they would split it before the ushers managed to escort them out. During the years following, that church experienced splits and new pastors one after the other.

I realized, emphatically, that angels are there to deliver us. But they are looking for us to do something too. They wait for our prayers and determination to stand in the authority of God. That is why we have to be persistent about prayer and things of the spirit. Otherwise we risk allowing the enemy to have access.

FALL DOWN AND GET DELIVERED

The story of three Hebrew boys who stood up to a king and an entire nation devoted to idolatry is found in Daniel 3. These young men—Shadrach, Meshach, and Abednego—stood up for God, and stood up for their faith in His delivering power.

Even though they were men full of faith in God, could they have been thinking, "How could this be happening? Are we really sentenced to death?" They didn't speak it aloud, but their minds probably turned to consider the experience of dying in a blazing fire. Confident they had done the right thing, though, they still could not believe what was about to take place. Was God going to let it happen?

In verse 15, King Nebuchadnezzar taunted them by saying, "What god will be able to rescue you from my hand?" (NIV). Surely, the almighty

God would not allow them to be thrown to their deaths without doing something. Was God going to stop this horrible sentencing? As things continued to move forward, it didn't appear so.

King Nebuchadnezzar had sentenced them to the furnace because they refused to worship an idol. These heroes decided they were not going to betray the Lord. They refused to bow to the idol.

But just before their execution, the king provided them one last opportunity to join with the other idol worshipers of the day. They responded with refusal by saying:

> Our God whom we serve is able to deliver us from the burning fiery furnace, and He will deliver us from your hand, O king. But if not, let it be known to you, O king, that we do not serve your gods, nor will we worship the gold image which you have set up.
> —Daniel 3:17–18, NKJV

"And Nebuchadnezzar was furious with Shadrach, Meshach and Abednego, and his attitude toward them changed" (verse 19, NIV). Yes, his attitude changed. He was outraged that they had again refused to worship the statue he erected. The New King James Version says King Nebuchadnezzar was so angry he was "full of fury." So the king ordered that the boys be thrown into the fiery furnace—and he had the furnace they were to be thrown into heated seven times hotter than normal.

Seven times hotter! Who could escape it? Who could live through it? Daniel 3:22 says the flames were so hot, they even killed the soldiers who threw Shadrach, Meshach, and Abednego into the fire. Then verses 23–25 tell us that as they fell down in the furnace, the Son of God appeared in the flames with them. Their fall to the ground was more than the effect of the heat. It was an example to us that their worship was directed to the right place.

When Scripture says Shadrach, Meshach, and Abednego fell into the fire, the words "fell down" in the Hebrew is the word *naphal*. The Hebrew lexicon says the definition of *nephal* is "to fall down, to fall prostrate, to prostrate one's self, and to lie prostrate." Instead of falling before a man-made statue as the king had said to do, they fell down in the middle of the fire before the Son of God!

As the story goes, they were supernaturally unharmed by the flames because they didn't change their convictions—even when they felt incredible pressure to quit. Their devoted worship to God delivered them even when the heat was on—literally!

They were delivered so completely that even after being in the middle of the flames, "...the fire had not touched them. Not a hair on their heads was singed, and their clothing was not scorched. They didn't even smell of smoke!" (verse 27, NLT). If we will worship in the middle of our heated trials, we will undoubtedly see God's delivering power.

This is also why the devil tempted Jesus to worship him. Just after Jesus had been baptized and was led by the Holy Spirit into the wilderness, "the devil took Him up on an exceedingly high mountain, and showed Him all the kingdoms of the world and their glory. And he said to Him, 'All these things I will give You if You will fall down and worship me'" (Matthew 4:8–9, NKJV).

Satan wanted Jesus to bow down to him and thus stop the delivering power of the Son of God!

The devil wanted the same kind of worship from Jesus that the Hebrew boys gave the Son of God in the fiery furnace. He wanted Jesus to bow to him because that expression of worship speaks of complete devotion and commitment. He knew the highest form of worship was to bow to the ground.

This high form of worship is described in John 4:23–24. It uses the phrase "true worshippers," which means to literally bow and kiss the feet. This is what Satan was trying to get from Jesus and what King Nebuchadnezzar wanted from Shadrach, Meshach, and Abednego.

The reason this type of worship is mirrored throughout Scripture is because it expresses commitment. (See Nehemiah 8:6; Psalm 95:6; Revelation 4:10; 5:14; 7:11; 19:10.) It is an expressive worship that doesn't leave God alone and in return enjoys His delivering power. "When I cry unto thee, then shall mine enemies turn back: this I know; for God is for me" (Psalm 56:9). Our dedication to bow ourselves in worship from our hearts will call for the delivering power of the Lord in our present situation.

FREE FROM THE PRISON SPIRITS

> Some of you were locked in a dark cell, cruelly confined behind bars, punished for defying God's Word, for turning your back on the High God's counsel—a hard sentence, and your hearts so heavy, and not a soul in sight to help. Then you called out to God in your desperate condition; he got you out in the nick of time. He led you out of your dark, dark cell, broke open the jail and led you out. So thank God for his marvelous love, for his miracle mercy to the children he loves; He shattered the heavy jailhouse doors, he snapped the prison bars like matchsticks!
>
> —Psalm 107:10–16, The Message

Many people are bound to some form of prison cell in their life and desperately want to experience deliverance. Psalm 126:1 says God wants to turn your captivity whether it is hidden or outward and obvious. He wants to help you be free from whatever has you entangled. In some people's lives there are what we call "prison spirits" that keep people in a cell of defeat, bondage, oppression, and torment.

The Bible describes when Peter was in the middle of two soldiers—jailers or guards—while in prison by saying, "When Herod would have brought him forth, the same night Peter was sleeping between two soldiers, bound with two chains: and the keepers before the door kept the prison" (Acts 12:6). Now these soldiers or jailers were actual people, but Satan has "jailers" he uses to bind people.

You could be bound wrongfully to a person, of course, but the jailer spirit keeping you captive could also be a sin habit, demonic stronghold, generational curse, or private sin. The devil will assign these jailer or prison spirits to people so they can never seem to get free from bondage.

Generally, people already know what prison spirit is assigned to them and to what sin habit they are bound. In the case of Peter's natural prison experience, we can metaphorically see two types of bondages. He was bound between two chains, and there are two types of chains that bind people in the spirit.

The first chain represents inward and hidden bondage that is difficult for others to see. The second kind of bondage is the outward kind everyone knows about. Everyone who struggles with some type of bondage will struggle with one of these. Your freedom from a jailer spirit that wants to keep you bound begins with praise and worship.

Paul and Silas were freed from the prison when "at midnight Paul and Silas prayed, and sang praises unto God: and the prisoners heard them. And suddenly there was a great earthquake, so that the foundations of the prison were shaken: and immediately all the doors were opened, and every one's bands were loosed" (Acts 16:25–26). Of course, the most difficult time to praise God is when you feel the pain of bondage. You feel like a failure and are unable to break out. But in the atmosphere of praise there is freedom, because the act of worship places God higher than yourself. Worship exalts the Lord over your own failures and sins.

Paul and Silas praised God at midnight—their darkest hour. That means they praised God even when they didn't feel like doing it. Paul and Silas would have never been free if they would have left God alone in worship.

They didn't stay bound. Instead, they did exactly what the three Hebrew boys did—they worshiped. To God, their worship was a cry for deliverance and freedom from bondage and slavery. If people would just close their eyes and begin to enter into worship, things will begin to break off them.

Worship is one of the greatest ways to get free and stay free. Another example the Bible tells us about is in 1 Samuel when David worshiped God and evil spirits would leave King Saul. It was again in the atmosphere of worship that the evil spirits fled.

The same will happen for you if you will make a lifestyle of worship. When is the last time you worshiped the Lord privately and just cried out to Him that you want to be free? You must make times of worship to the Lord a priority. Once you do that, then you have to decide not to feed prison spirits. Remember that they are rulers of darkness. (See Ephesians 6:12.) You feed them by allowing them to rule because of your choices. When you give them darkness, they can rule you.

Here's an amusing but true example of how demons gain power over people: Have you noticed how the devil started out as only a snake in the Garden of Eden? But by the time you get to the Book of Revelation, he is a dragon. Someone had to be feeding him because he grew!

So decide to live a clean life and be proud to be a Christian. I am so honored to be a citizen of heaven, and I am proud to be a follower of Jesus. I want to please Him by my lifestyle and choices.

You can be free from prison spirits. You will find deliverance when you don't leave God alone in worship and by making godly choices.

THE ROAD TO BONDAGE

In Judges 13–16, we read the story of a man named Samson, to whom the Lord gave supernatural strength to defeat the enemy. God wants us to have this type of strength in the spirit to defeat the devil. And He wants us to live delivered so that we never lose it.

Samson, who was a Nazirite from his mother's womb, honored the vows of a Nazirite—vows of consecration, dedication, and purity before the Lord. A big problem Samson had was that places he went gave the appearance of him compromising his commitment. (See Judges 14:1–4.) Those choices made him progress from purity and liberty into a place of complete bondage.

His progression toward a stronghold began in the city of Timnath, which concordances give the Hebrew meaning as a "portion, allotment, or allotted portion." I believe that is the place where you feel convicted about your choices as you continue on your course of action.

Then Samson went to Gaza, a city which dictionaries and concordances show the meaning of as "the strong." We can see that because he ignored his early convictions and compromised anyhow, he ended up bound to a stronghold. (See Judges 16:16–21.)

The road to bondage was then becoming progressively worse in Samson's life. You will find in Judges 14:5–9 that he began regularly breaking his vows and even lying about it. We know that, ultimately, Samson ended up losing his entire anointing because his final compromise with a harlot named Delilah took him out! He lost his anointing and his strength.

The Philistines, which represent demon spirits, then bound him in chains and poked his eyes out. This is an example of how strongholds will cause us to live in spiritual blindness.

Samson did something, however, that will give hope to every person who has failed. Even when all seemed lost, he didn't give up. Although he completely failed the Lord, Samson was determined to try and correct what he had done wrong. Do you know that God honored him for it?

We see in Judges 16:23–25, Samson was brought to a party the Philistines gave to celebrate his captivity—they wanted him to stand before everyone so they could laugh at his defeat. That is right where the devil has a lot of people—even some Christians—and he is laughing at their defeat, the condition of their bondage, and their blindness.

I wanted to tell you this story so you will have hope to be delivered today. Perhaps your past choices were not God's best, and you wish you had not compromised in the decisions that you made. But Jesus loves you, and He wants to help you regardless of anything you have done.

In verses 25–26, we read how the Philistines put Samson between two pillars to make fun of him. While the Philistines were laughing at Samson, he asked a young boy to help him lean on those pillars because he wanted to pull them down. I believe those two pillars represent the strongholds and bondages that are in the middle of many people's lives—and they need to come down too.

Of course, we know how Samson's story ends. When he pushed on the pillars, once again receiving supernatural strength, the house came down and killed all the people inside—including Samson. The Bible, however, says Samson killed more in his death than in his life. (See Judges 16:27–30.) God honored his repentance and his heart to make amends for his prior wrongdoing.

The lesson of Samson is that he didn't give up even though he blew it terribly. But he refused to leave God alone until he corrected his error. For Samson, this was his deliverance. Regardless of what binds you today, God will honor your repentance and your determination for deliverance. He will help you place your hands on the "pillars" and tear down the strongholds in your life.

ONE MORE DAY WITH THE FROGS

We have power over the devil to cast him out of both our lives and the lives of others. Some people, however, want to stay bound, and they like their demonic strongholds—they just don't like the pain and suffering bondage produces. Rather than working toward being delivered, they choose "one more day with the frogs."

One more day with the frogs comes from the time when the children of Israel were in bondage in Egypt and the Lord brought the plague of frogs on Pharaoh and the land. (See Exodus 8:1–15.) In verse 8, Pharaoh called for Moses and Aaron and told them that he would let the people of Israel go if the plague of frogs would just end. "You set the time!" Moses replied. "Tell me when you want me to pray for you, your officials, and your people. Then you and your houses will be rid of the frogs."

Do you know Pharaoh's response?

He said tomorrow! Not right now, not as soon as you can, but tomorrow!

He wanted another day with his frogs. And one more day with the frogs is the attitude many people have regarding the bondage they are living in. They want to keep it just a little longer.

Pharaoh's mistake was that keeping his "bondage" a little longer resulted in the downfall of the kingdom. What you put off today may be your downfall tomorrow.

I knew a couple who were dating and, at the time, attended our church, who did the same thing. The Lord kept giving me dreams that they were compromising their lives sexually and using drugs. So I called both of them into my office—because the Lord wouldn't have given me the dreams if He didn't want me to do anything about it. Jesus wants clean local churches, where people live pure.

At first they denied what I told them I had seen in the dreams, until I started to give them specific details about what the Lord had shown me. I even named the place where I saw them go and what they did there.

Immediately the woman began to cry, saying, "You are a true man of God, Pastor. God is truly speaking to you." She admitted to everything. And although he was cornered, the man would not repent or acknowledge the truth in my dreams. I told them that their relationship was not a healthy one and it would be best if they broke it off. The woman, of course, agreed it would be for the best, but she wasn't sure she could make a commitment to end it right then. She needed another day to think about it—one more day with the frogs!

Her one more day wound up costing her. She stayed with this man and paid a heavy price for it, to say the least. I saw her years later, and I didn't even recognize her. She was completely addicted to drugs and suffered from pain and abuse. Her one more day of bondage was destroying her life.

Frogs are compared to demons in scripture. Revelation 16:13–14 says, "And I saw three unclean spirits like frogs come out of the mouth of the dragon, and out of the mouth of the beast, and out of the mouth of the false prophet. For they are the spirits of devils, working miracles, which go forth unto the kings of the earth and of the whole world, to gather them to the battle of that great day of God Almighty."

Do you want to spend one more day with the frogs, or will you refuse to leave God alone until deliverance is manifest? You do not have to live with prison spirits or with the frogs. You can be free today if you will determine that you will not leave God alone regarding your deliverance.

My phone rang late one evening. Someone on the other line informed me that they had a friend locked in their basement and this friend was manifesting a demon. At that time, I wasn't even a pastor. I was just a young Christian. Trying to help my friend, I went to the house. I arrived only to hear the noise of demonic screams downstairs. We went down the steps and saw a man on the floor, moving his head back and forth. I immediately commanded those evil spirits to come out of him. It took a few minutes, but then he was restored to himself.

Later when I talked with the young man, he told me that he just wanted to be free. He had such a determination to be free. Because of that, the evil spirits left him immediately. He didn't want another day with the frogs!

LOOSE YOURSELF

Scripture says in Isaiah 52:2, "Shake thyself from the dust; arise, and sit down, O Jerusalem: loose thyself from the bands of thy neck, O captive daughter of Zion." You might be thinking there is no hope for you. Regardless of what you are facing, you can be free. Refuse to leave God alone about your deliverance. Rise up, shake yourself, and be determined that this is what you want. Darkness can't dwell with light. Demons hate righteousness, and God's anointing power breaks every yoke and undoes every heavy burden in your life.

> And it shall come to pass in that day, that his burden shall be taken away from off thy shoulder, and his yoke from off thy neck, and the yoke shall be destroyed because of the anointing.
>
> —Isaiah 10:27

I always encourage the people of our church to come to every service and even bring other people that need help. It was the same in Jesus's meetings, and it is the same way today, that where His power is, people are being set free.

If you follow the simple principles below, you can enjoy a life of God's promises and watch the strongholds of the devil be broken from your life. These things will help you target your focus and place your hands on the pillars of liberty.

- Refuse to leave God alone (Jeremiah 33:3).
- Use the Word of God and the name of Jesus (Matthew 8:16).
- Always believe the Lord wants you to be free.
- Stand your ground (Ephesians 6:13).
- Refuse to give up on your deliverance (2 Timothy 4:7).
- Stay in church with an anointed pastor who will help you.

Jesus wants you to be free. John 8:36 says, "If the Son sets you free, you are truly free" (NLT). God has been waiting to deliver you; just refuse to leave Him alone. He is not ignoring you or refusing to deliver you—He wants to help you. He is waiting for you to cry out, put your hands on the pillar like Samson, and bow down and worship Him like the three Hebrew boys. The result will be your enemies turning back and you being free.

Why? God is for you, He is faithful, and He wants to deliver you!

6

I WILL NOT LEAVE YOU ALONE
UNTIL YOUR POWER COMES

And so it happened. They were walking along and talking.
Suddenly a chariot and horses of fire came between them
and Elijah went up in a whirlwind to heaven. Elisha
saw it all and shouted, "My father, my father! You—the
chariot and cavalry of Israel!" When he could no longer
see anything, he grabbed his robe and ripped it to pieces.
Then he picked up Elijah's cloak that had fallen from him,
returned to the shore of the Jordan, and stood there. He
took Elijah's cloak—all that was left of Elijah!—and hit
the river with it, saying, "Now where is the God of Elijah?
Where is he?" When he struck the water, the river divided
and Elisha walked through.

—2 Kings 2:11–14, THE MESSAGE

WHERE IS THE God of Elijah?" This was the cry from a son
named Elisha, who deeply loved his spiritual father Elijah.
In 2 Kings 2, we find a powerful story of spiritual sonship
and the love that Elisha had for Elijah and the God he served.

Elijah was preparing to leave the earth, and he brought this prophet,
whom he had mentored from the city of Gilgal, and said something
very unusual to him: "Tarry here, I pray thee; for the LORD hath sent
me to Bethel. And Elisha said unto him, As the LORD liveth, and as

thy soul liveth, I will not leave thee. So they went down to Bethel" (verse 2). In other words, Elisha said, "Listen, as long as you are alive, I am not going to leave you. So I am coming with you to Bethel." This same scenario repeats three more times, and each time Elisha refused to leave the man of God.

Why did it seem as though the prophet Elijah was trying to discourage his spiritual son from following him? It seems like such an odd response for someone who is about to leave. Naturally, if I had been Elijah, I could picture myself sitting down with my successor trying to give him all the last-minute words of wisdom necessary to help him carry out his future tasks. Yet here is Elijah, acting as though he is trying to get rid of him.

Regardless of how many times Elijah tried, Elisha was not going to give up. It seemed like Elijah wanted to be alone. But every time Elisha refused to leave, his spiritual father and mentor, Elijah, gave in to him. It is as if he was looking for something.

Did he really want Elisha to go away? No! Without question, he was testing Elisha's resolve and commitment—he was trying to provoke a response. If Elisha showed that he was truly committed to his spiritual father, then it would also show that he would appreciate the anointing and the ministry he was about to inherit. If he would follow him and love him, he would also love the mantle of power about to be passed on to him. Otherwise, he may have only wanted the power to promote his own purpose.

Once Elisha's level of hunger was evident, Elijah left in a whirlwind. That is when Elisha was ready to receive the mantle of anointing from his spiritual father. He was positioned to receive the blessing because he had refused to leave Elijah alone. This was what he was crying out for and had always loved so much about his mentor—he carried the power of God!

It was dear to his heart to embrace that same kind of anointing. You can almost feel the emotion as his spiritual father was taken away. As he watched Elijah go, Elisha cried out, "My father, my father!..." (verse 12). He had been so resolute about following this man, even when he tried to discourage him. Now in one final, desperate moment, he reached toward his father and cried, even as Elijah left him for the last time.

Once Elijah was gone, all that remained was the coat he had been wearing—his mantle, the very symbol of the God who had anointed him. Elisha just wanted God to be inside of the coat the way He was when Elijah wore it. He wanted God to rest upon him the way He had upon his mentor—so he could be like the man he loved.

It is a touching moment as we see how this prophet embraced his new responsibility and picked up the mantle of Elijah. As soon as he touched it, he cried out from his soul, "Where is the LORD God of Elijah?" (verse 14). Maybe he thought, "Oh, if only God were here the same way He was for Elijah." What he didn't know was that his refusal to leave his father resulted in him being clothed with the same power. He had pursued his father and now had received his same mighty anointing.

Elisha didn't leave Elijah alone until he had received the power that had been on his life. We have to honestly ask ourselves, what are we willing to do in order to walk in the power of God? It is our refusal, as sons and daughters of God, to leave our Father alone that holds the key to power in our lives. Elisha's refusal deposited the necessary ingredients into his life, enabling him to step into some big shoes and carry on a powerful ministry.

During the time when Elisha followed Elijah, in 2 Kings 2:1–7, he went to four places: Gilgal, Bethel, Jericho, and Jordan. Each one of these cities represented a different test of his heart and commitment, determining his ability to walk in that power. He would need to pass each test, which would make him the kind of man who would not give up until God's miracle power manifests in every situation.

As we study the remainder of this chapter, we will see how important the tests become in making *us* men and women who will not leave God alone until we walk in His power. God is looking to build something in people so they won't stop pursuing Him until His power comes.

Go to the Hospital and Rock the Baby in the Chair

All of us must come to a place where we, like Elisha, have to decide if we will be dedicated to seeing God's power. Sometimes it is easier to just stop pursuing when the going gets tough or it doesn't look like God is responding to us. To Elisha it may have looked like the power of God left in the whirlwind, but he just needed to grab ahold of it.

He had been prepared for it. He had passed all the tests. Now he would just have to use that same determination to walk in it himself. That is what we have to decide too: whether we are determined to walk in God's power ourselves.

To give an example of this, I walked through a situation with a family in our church who had just had a baby girl. Doctors were reporting that the baby's blood-platelet count was extremely low. They were very concerned if this newborn was even going to live. They needed a miracle. She was diagnosed with an incurable disease that attacked her liver and blood. Her liver was failing, and doctors were very negative, saying she had only an 11 percent chance of living.

As a church, we rose up to pray, but still things continued to get worse. For days we saw very little results. Maybe this is how Elisha felt when he was not certain if God's power would be there for him the way it had been for Elijah. It seemed like God was ignoring us while this little girl lay almost lifeless in the incubator. Regardless of the outlook, we kept speaking God's promises of healing.

Finally, within myself, I just determined that this was not right. God was going to do a miracle, and we were not going to have it any other way! I became determined, and the child's parents and others were determined with me. There was just something that rose in us and put previous fear and shock about the situation aside.

The next Sunday morning, I heard the Holy Spirit speak to me and say, "Hank, go rock that baby in the chair."

I knew it was the Lord, so I called the parents, and they immediately arranged it so I could rock their little girl. I felt in my heart that something had turned in the spirit. On the way to the hospital, I thanked the Lord for His power. There was going to be nothing less than the power of God.

In the hospital, I rocked that child under the anointing. This time I could feel the power of God. I don't even remember praying anything special. I just said, "Lord, You have healed this baby, now let Your power manifest."

Miraculously the next day, the doctors were amazed at the blood-platelet count and significant changes in her. She suddenly started getting better, and today she is a healthy, adorable little girl who is full of God's life.

What made the difference? I believe we decided that we *had to have* the power of God—we were going to pursue and find it. Just like Elisha, who refused to leave his spiritual father alone until his power came, we refused to leave our heavenly Father alone until *His* power came. And, praise the Lord, it did!

FROM THE FOUR PLACES OF TESTING INTO THE POWER OF GOD

Also like Elisha, our determination toward God's healing power for this baby was built by four ingredients—the backbone for why we could hold on to the power of God. In 2 Kings 2, when Elisha followed Elijah from Gilgal to Jordan, something was gradually building inside of him. He was experiencing four places of testing where, in each place he went, it was making a man who would forever know how to grab ahold of the power of God and never let it go.

Gilgal

Gilgal was the first place of testing for Elisha during the last days he was with Elijah. This could have possibly been the first place they traveled to, but the Bible only records them leaving it. Gilgal represents, however, the "place of new beginnings" in the life of the hungry believer. The word *Gilgal* actually means "the rolling or a place rolled away." It is the picture of total conversion. The fruit of our lives when we have crossed into Gilgal should be that we are devoted to God and His ways. Gilgal will accomplish several things in our lives:

1. *God's kingdom is established.* Gilgal is the first place where we establish God's kingdom for ourselves. It is about God's government taking rule in our lives. It is the place where we become committed. Elisha had to be established in Gilgal to show he was submitted and committed. When Israel first entered the Promised Land at Gilgal, they immediately set up twelve stones representing God's kingdom government being established in them. (See Joshua 4:20.)

2. *Remove the old to prepare for the new.* Gilgal is the place where we cut away our fleshly habits that keep us from the power of God. Elisha also had to show that he could discipline his flesh. When Israel came to Gilgal, the Lord told Joshua to circumcise the people a second time (Joshua 5:2). In the spiritual circumcision of the heart, we cut away the fleshly areas to become like Jesus.

3. *Past influence is removed.* Joshua 5:9 says that Gilgal was the place where God removed the effects of Egypt from Israel. Elisha also came through Gilgal to show that he was not held back or intimidated by the past, but always moving forward. When God rolls away our reproach, the past no longer holds us back.

4. *More spiritual responsibility is required.* Gilgal is also the place of personal responsibility to grow spiritually. Elisha had to show himself responsible to follow Elijah. For Israel, Gilgal was the place where God's heavenly manna stopped (Joshua 5:10–12). God was making them take responsibility. It was no longer just a heavenly handout every day; they had to grow and look for God to bless them in new ways.

Bethel

After Gilgal, Elisha had to enter Bethel. Bethel was the place of prayer. The name *Bethel* in Hebrew means "house of God." It is here that Abram met with God and built an altar, and it was also where Jacob saw his vision of God's presence with the ladder that reached to heaven. Bethel is the place where we develop our prayer life and our place in the body of Christ. Bethel will accomplish several things in our lives:

1. *A connection to the church.* Bethel represents the house of God that is us, the church. It also speaks of the actual local church. Bethel is the place where we are developed to become solid members among God's people. First Timothy 3:15 says, "I write so that you may know how you ought to conduct yourself in the house of God, which is the church of the living God, the pillar and ground of the truth" (NKJV). Elisha had to experience

Bethel so he could be a stable man who could be trusted with the mantle. Also at the church of Antioch, the apostles received training so they could properly represent the gospel. (See Acts 13:1.) Bethel helps us become people who can act right among God's people and be a pillar of support in the church.

2. *A personal revelation and experience.* When Elisha came through Bethel, it was also so he could have his own personal experience with God. It wasn't enough to ride on the experience of Elijah. Bethel will develop in you a personal revelation and walk with God. Jacob also experienced Bethel. Genesis 28:16, 19 says, "And Jacob awaked out of his sleep, and he said, Surely the LORD is in this place; and I knew it not....And he called the name of that place Bethel."

3. *A committed prayer life.* Bethel is what develops in you a lifestyle that won't live without prayer. If Elisha was going to be God's prophet, he would need a commitment to prayer. Without prayer, you will not have the power or fuel you need to do what God has purposed for your life. Bethel is your place of prayer.

I want to share a few additional things about Bethel because it is such a significant place to experience with God. I am so thankful for God walking me through many experiences at Bethel because it was what prepared me for ministry. Through it, God matured me to be a blessing in the kingdom of God. I love Bethel because it also develops in you the ability to rely on God when there is no one but you and Him. That kind of relationship prepares you for Jericho like nothing else because, when you're facing a trial, the Lord's face is your sustaining force.

Elisha was going to have to deal with some battles alone, with no one to depend on but God. Without a Bethel experience, he would not have had that confidence. Bethel is a personal experience of maturity, dependence on God, and prayer.

Jericho

Then Elisha had to come to Jericho. This was the place of battle where God first gave Israel victory in the land of Canaan. It was where the intimidating walls of resistance were broken down and victory was given to the people. And it is an important place where we learn about walking in the power of God.

If Elisha was going to walk in God's power, he would have to know how to deal with resistance. Jericho is where we confront the powers of darkness and become strong in the spirit. It is the place of battle and victory and demonstrating God's power. Jericho will do several things in us:

1. *Develop an overcoming spirit.* David could defeat Goliath because the Lord had taught him to fight by first defeating both the lion and the bear. The lion and the bear represent both the outward and inward battles we face. God will require us to stay in Jericho so we develop an overcoming spirit to defeat the enemy. When David received the revelation that he could defeat both the lion and the bear, he didn't hesitate to take on Goliath. He became a confident overcomer no matter what the challenge.

2. *Deliver us.* To fulfill God's purpose for us, we need to be delivered from darkness. Bears speak of inward battles because bears feed, hibernate, and then come out of hiding in the next season. This time they are hungrier

than before and looking again for something to fill them. While they seem to be gone for a season, they suddenly reappear. Remember, suppressing something in your life is not genuine deliverance. We need to experience Jericho to be truly delivered from the bear and overcome the evil spirits that bind us.

3. *Teach us about the power of God.* Lions are the outward, obvious battles we face. They come suddenly to consume us. (See 1 Peter 5:8.) When you learn to wield your spiritual weapons and rise up to defeat outward attacks in your life, you learn how to walk in God's power. Lions like to roar against you to make you feel powerless. But once you learn to operate in the anointing to defeat the enemy, the devil cannot destroy you.

Jordan

Jordan is the place of crossing. It is where you step into your heavenly inheritance the same way that Elisha did when he picked up the mantle of Elijah and parted the Jordan. It is the place where you finally cross over and step into God's purpose for your life. It wasn't enough for Elisha to stay at the place where he saw Elijah leave; he had to step into the new place God had for him. He had to cross the Jordan and go forward.

Jordan speaks of always moving, always progressing. When it is time to step into Jordan, you will know because the mantle will fall to you. God will use people and leaders to give you a mantle to carry across your Jordan. Elisha didn't cross Jordan until he came through the other place and then received the anointing by following the lead of another. By faith, you can step into your Jordan today. Simply use the many tools God placed in you, pick up the mantle, and move into your divine blessing. It requires a choice—but there you will always find the blessing of God.

God the Father will continually bring us to certain places in our lives like Gilgal, Bethel, Jericho, and Jordan to position us for His power. If you are continually willing to experience them, you will be made ready to experience the supernatural power of God.

Yes, like Elisha, it takes commitment to stay with it in the places of testing. His four testing places produced powerful miracles in his life, and I believe these experiences will produce the same for you today. The key was that he had to decide whether or not he was going to leave Elijah alone—even when it seemed like he had every reason to go back. Nothing stopped him from pursuing his spiritual father to the four places of testing. He didn't stop pursuing until he received the power!

What might happen if we pursued our heavenly Father this way? What might happen if we allowed His Spirit to bring us to the four places of testing and we embraced them wholeheartedly instead of reverting back in fear? I believe the result will be that we will see God's miracles, glory, and power work in our lives. Don't leave God alone—pursue Him until His power comes!

TWELVE BLESSINGS OF PURSUING THE FATHER

Once Elisha walked through the places of testing, he began to walk in some of the most incredible miracles recorded in the Bible. This is the power received when we don't leave God alone. Here are twelve of Elisha's miracles that I believe are similar to what God wants us to experience when we pursue Him:

1. *The river Jordan parted* (2 Kings 2:14–15). You will cross over into your inheritance, your dream of experiencing

God's power. You will be living proof of the anointing of God.

2. *The salt and the river* (2 Kings 2:19–22). The water was bad, and Elisha put salt in the water to heal it. You will have power to heal that which is cursed.

3. *The children and the two she bears* (2 Kings 2:23–24). Children spoke against the prophet Elisha, and he spoke a curse on them with his words. While this miracle of Elisha produced a horrible end, it also reveals the power to prophesy with our words and see them come to pass.

4. *The valley of ditches* (2 Kings 3:11, 16, 21–23). The people sought out Elisha for a miracle. The ditches would be filled with water without wind or rain filling them. When it looks like you are in a ditch or rut, God will make a way for you supernaturally.

5. *The oil that multiplied* (2 Kings 4:1–7). A widow woman owed money to the creditors and couldn't pay her debt. She came to Elisha, who told her to borrow as many pitchers as possible, and the oil was multiplied in the pitchers. This will also be the result for us—the oil of God's Spirit will stay on us, and it will be a continual supply. Our needs will be met in abundance.

6. *The barren woman who received a child* (2 Kings 4:8–17). Elisha prophesied that a barren woman would have a child. When we seek our heavenly Father, we will prophesy things that will come to pass—barren things will bear fruit.

7. *A dead son brought to life* (2 Kings 4:32–37). After the barren woman had a son, the boy later died. The woman came to Elisha still believing all was well. Elisha, with God's power, raised the boy back to life. The power of God on your life will help bring dead things back to life for yourself and others.

8. *Poison in the pot* (2 Kings 4:38–41). Elisha cast some meal cake into a pot of poisoned stew and the poison was neutralized. The power of God in you will render ineffective the things that the enemy uses to poison our lives and the lives of others.

9. *An axe head restored* (2 Kings 6:1–7). An axe head was separated from the handle as the sons of the prophets were chopping wood, and it fell into the river. Elisha, with the power of God, caused the axe head to float and reconnected it. God will place us at the cutting edge of what He wants to build in others, His church, and us.

10. *Opening the eyes of his servant to see in the spirit* (2 Kings 6:15–17). When Israel was surrounded by a great army, Elisha caused the eyes of his servant to be opened into the spirit so he could see they were protected by a heavenly army greater than that of their enemy. God will help us see prophetically and supernaturally so we can win great battles for Him.

11. *The prophet, the king, and the arrow* (2 Kings 13:14–19). Elisha put his hands and the hands of the king of Israel together and told him to smite the ground with an arrow. The number of times the king smote the ground would

determine the Lord's victory against the enemy. The Lord will anoint us to win battles completely—not just some of the battle, but total victory.

12. *The dead bones and the dead man* (2 Kings 13:20–21). Elisha had died and was buried with the anointing still in his bones. When a dead man was thrown in the same grave as Elisha, the man came back to life. God is going to anoint us so we can supernaturally impart the power of God to future generations.

As Long as My Soul Lives

In every place of testing, the request from Elijah to Elisha was, "You wait here, while I leave without you." He didn't want to leave Elisha; it was a test to provoke a response and reveal Elisha's heart.

Now while the example of Elijah and Elisha is a picture of God and our response to Him, we can also see others on whom God waited for their response. We saw it with Moses, and we can also see it with the children of Israel. God tested their hearts in the wilderness. Deuteronomy 8:2 says, "You shall remember that the LORD your God led you all the way these forty years in the wilderness, to humble you and test you, to know what was in your heart, whether you would keep His commandments or not" (NKJV).

The Lord said He literally tested them and humbled them just to see what was in their hearts. What would be their response? Similar to how Elijah kept putting Elisha off, it seemed to them as if God was going to let them die in the wilderness and was ignoring their predicaments. The real truth was that the Lord was waiting to see what they would do. Elijah was waiting to see what Elisha would do, and today God waits to see what we will do.

It might seem to you as if God is off somewhere, not interested in your current situation. That is not the case! He is waiting. Just as Elijah did with his spiritual son, Elisha, God just wants to see that you will pursue Him and not give up. He wants to hear His people say—He wants to hear you say—"As long as my soul lives, I will not leave you!"

Matthew 12:34 says, "Out of the abundance of the heart the mouth speaketh." We can determine what a person thinks or feels in their heart by what comes from their mouth. The children of Israel complained in the wilderness when they were tested. Their heart spoke just what they really felt. On the other hand, the heart attitude and verbal response of Elisha, the spiritual son, was, "As the LORD liveth, and as thy soul liveth, I will not leave thee" (2 Kings 2:6). In other words, "It may seem like You are not there, God, or that You aren't hearing my prayer. But mark it down. I refuse to leave You alone. I will follow You wherever You go."

PRIVATE PRAYER PRODUCES PUBLIC POWER

Once we determine that no matter what the circumstance, we will pursue God, we have to stay in prayer as He leads us through the places of testing. Otherwise we will never stay with it and ultimately never enjoy the miraculous power God has for us. Private prayer will always produce public power in your life.

This was the way it was in Jesus's life. You read how, many times, He prayed all day or all night, alone with God. He would finish praying and immediately the power of God was in manifestation. People were healed, delivered, and blessed as a result. Look how His private prayer life thrust Him into public power.

- *Jesus prayed:* "And he withdrew himself into the wilderness, and prayed" (Luke 5:16).

- *The result:* "And, behold, men brought in a bed a man which was taken with a palsy: and they sought means to bring him in, and to lay him before him. And when they could not find by what way they might bring him in because of the multitude, they went upon the housetop, and let him down through the tiling with his couch into the midst before Jesus" (Luke 5:18–19).

- *Jesus prayed:* "And it came to pass in those days, that he went out into a mountain to pray, and continued all night in prayer to God" (Luke 6:12).

- *The result:* "And they that were vexed with unclean spirits: and they were healed. And the whole multitude sought to touch him: for there went virtue out of him, and healed them all" (Luke 6:18–19).

Prayer is the secret weapon of power. So many times, before Jesus manifested a miracle, you see He spent time in prayer. One time while I was preaching at a conference, there were thousands of people in the auditorium, and some were commenting that the power of God was so strong. In fact, the ushers in the hallways were even falling under God's power, and people, by whole sections, were falling and shaking with the anointing. Many said they had never felt power like that. I remembered spending extra time fasting and praying before that conference. So when I went out into the open public, the power of God hit.

Why? It was all because of prayer!

Whenever Jesus or the apostles would depart to be alone with God, they were always seen later operating in tremendous power. Jesus even told us, "When you pray, go into your room, and when you have shut your door, pray to your Father who is in the secret place; and your Father who sees in secret will reward you openly" (Matthew 6:6, NKJV). In other words, when we take time to not leave God alone and put everything else on hold, He is saying there is an open reward for doing it. He will reward us with His supernatural power. We will see His power show up as well as many other wonderful blessings. Private prayer produces public results.

We can see this principle again in Luke 4, when Jesus is led into the wilderness to be tempted of the devil. He had spent time alone with God, so when He was later tempted, His private prayer life taught Him how to overcome the devil and temptation. He then came out of that wilderness with power as a result: "And Jesus returned in the power of the Spirit into Galilee: and there went out a fame of him through all the region round about" (Luke 4:14).

I find that time alone with God, and shutting off every distraction, is the key to God's power manifesting in my life. Having your own private time and place is important. I have had every kind of "prayer closet" you can imagine. I have prayed in fields, forests, garages, tents, wood cabins, and even small sheds, to name a few. I have also prayed in my car and sometimes looked over to realize people were looking at me strangely while I prayed. If that happens to you, just act like you are talking on your cell phone—they will never know that you have God on the line. I am determined that, no matter what, I am going to keep pursuing Him in a place of prayer so that I can be used in His power.

Positioning yourself for power through prayer also takes obedience and requires sacrifice. First Kings 18:25–29 says there were four things that the prophets of Baal did to try to get an answer from their god. But their efforts produced no power. While they worshiped a false god, their example paints a picture of why many Christians don't have power, even though they serve the true Lord. In their effort to produce power, they placed the offering to their false god on their altar and did four specific things:

1. They dressed their offering (verse 25).
2. They leaped (verse 26).
3. They cried aloud (verse 28).
4. They prophesied (verse 29).

Notice that although they dressed, leaped, cried, and even prophesied, there was still no power or answer to their prayers. They appeared to do all the right "ritualistic" things, but they called on a false god with no power. Today, many Christians do these same things before the one and true God, Jesus Christ. They dress up every Sunday, leap, cry out, and even prophesy. But remember, even though all of these are great before God, unless they are done in faith, obedience, and sacrifice, backed up by a lifestyle of prayer, they will have no power.

I remember once, after just getting home from a long day at work, I lay on my bed and began to pray. I immediately felt God's presence and continued to pray through early evening. I kept seeing faces as I would pray. I kept praying and interceding for quite a while until, later that evening, I went on an outing with a street witnessing team. While we were out on the streets, I kept seeing people's faces flashing before my heart. It was just like what I saw when I was praying.

I walked into a national pizza chain that was full of high school football players and some parents after a game. I had never met any of them, but I noticed a big football player arm wrestling at a table. Almost the whole place was watching this young man arm wrestle. He stood up and looked around and asked, in a very prideful way, who was going to be the next challenger. Still today, I am amazed that out of my mouth came, "I am." I was a single man—I couldn't cook much either, so, as you can imagine, I was skin and bones—and barely twenty years old. But I had spent a lot of time fasting and praying. There was no way I could naturally beat this guy. In fact, when I sat down to arm wrestle this football player, he mocked me and called me "stick boy."

The game was on. I had an audience as people laughed at this David-and-Goliath match—he being Goliath and me being little David.

Then, with some kind of supernatural boldness, I told everyone that if I won, they had to listen to what I had to say. The team of people who came with me to witness were standing there with their eyes wide, expecting my certain defeat. People started to count down and then yelled, "Begin!"

I started to push his hand and arm and actually started gaining some when he stood up. He grabbed his hand and started to yell, "Hey, what do you have in your hand?" As I showed him my hand I said, "I don't have anything." He said he felt something like electricity shock him and go through him. He was sure I had some sort of shocking device in my hand. But the only shock I had was the power of the anointing. I knew it was the anointing, and I truly believe had he not stood up, the might of God would have enabled me to beat him.

He didn't continue, just in case stick boy might beat the big boy. God used it though, and I asked everyone to listen to what I had to say. Almost everyone in the place, including the workers, came to hear me preach the gospel. It was my refusal to leave God alone and crying out for His power that caused a sign and wonder that day. I had positioned myself in prayer earlier in the day, and the result was that the Lord brought His power. All those faces I had seen in prayer, I am convinced, were those I ministered to that night. God's power will come if you will sacrifice in prayer and pursue Him.

PRAY UNTIL THE RAIN COMES

If you pursue, pray, obey, and sacrifice, then there is one more secret to might and power in the spirit. It is called *persistence*. Elijah knew the importance of persistence too. In 1 Kings 18, he put his head between his knees seven times to pray for rain. This was not because he was getting into the crash position but rather the power position!

Once again, notice it took seven times before it seemed his answer came. It seemed that God wasn't answering him or was ignoring him. But to provoke a response from Elijah, and because of his position of persistence, it positioned him for a blessing. The blessing that came to Elijah was that of answered prayer—in the form of a cloud. It only started out as the size of a man's hand, but the continued prayer of Elijah turned this little hand of blessing into the outpouring of God. The Lord is always in a position to bless your life, but He is waiting for your persistent request from the earth so the clouds of blessing can rain over you.

When Elijah prayed, not only was there a cloud the size of a man's hand, but also there was the sound of an abundance of rain. For the hand of God to appear and bring the rain of answered prayer, we have to assume a position like Elijah's position. We have to be persistent in the position of prayer.

All of us have a rain cloud of blessing we can tap into. When you do, God's blessing will come as the rain and pour out on you. Ecclesiastes 11:3 says, "If the clouds are full, they pour out rain upon the earth" (NAS). If you want God's blessing to rain down on you, then you fill your rain cloud of blessing by prayer. The Bible also says we can have heavenly rains and fruitful seasons in our lives: "He did good, and gave us rain from heaven, and fruitful seasons, filling our hearts with food and gladness" (Acts 14:17).

It is always God's desire to bless His people, and He wants you to live under a spiritual rain cloud of His blessing. When God created Adam and Eve, the first thing He did was "God blessed them" (Genesis 1:28). How do we get our rain cloud to pour down blessings on us? Just as there are bank accounts on the earth, you can think of your rain cloud as a heavenly bank account. When the account is full, there is something to withdraw. Your rain cloud is filled with rain through your sacrifice and your persistent prayers. This cycle is why earthly rain is sometimes likened to prayer. Heavenly rain comes when we fill our clouds with spiritual "moisture." When they are full, they release the rain—the blessing of God.

Have you ever noticed how little it rains in the desert? The reason is because there is no moisture coming up from the ground to form rain clouds. In the same way, some people are not coming into steady blessing because they are in a desert of no sacrifice and little prayer. They are giving nothing to fill their rain cloud. Luke 6:38 says, "Give, and it shall be given unto you; good measure, pressed down, and shaken together, and running over, shall men give into your bosom. For with the same measure that ye mete withal it shall be measured to you again." Getting your rain cloud to become full is a continual process. It takes persistence.

If you have ever filled up water balloons, you soon realize the more water you put in the balloon, the more impact it has when you release it. When I was a kid, we used to have water balloon fights, and I was the one always getting soaked. I was more into filling the balloon fast while failing to get enough water into it. Then I would throw them, doing only a little damage to my foes. My opponents were mostly dry after we were finished, while I would be drenched, sloshing around in my shoes as I walked. Why? They realized that the more water they put in the balloon, the more water was released on impact.

It is the same way when filling up your spiritual bank account or heavenly rain cloud. As you give to the Lord in prayer, and give sacrificially in other ways, your rain cloud will get bigger and bigger. Like those water balloons, it will splash you with a great impact of blessings until you are walking around, sloshing in the blessings of God—they will overtake you!

Decide today that you will become like Elisha, who pursued even when he could have found a reason to quit. He followed his father into the place of testing, and the result was finding the blessing and power of God. If you are committed to it, you will see yourself manifest miracles and all the blessings God wants to make available to you. Be sure to make prayer your priority so you can enjoy the manifestation of power. Determine that you won't leave God alone until His power comes!

7

I Will Not Leave You Alone Until This Mountain Moves

> But Moses told the people, "Don't be afraid. Just stand still and watch the LORD rescue you today. The Egyptians you see today will never be seen again. The LORD himself will fight for you. Just stay calm." Then the LORD said to Moses, "Why are you crying out to me? Tell the people to get moving! Pick up your staff and raise your hand over the sea. Divide the water so the Israelites can walk through the middle of the sea on dry ground."
>
> —Exodus 14:13–16, NLT

ALTHOUGH HE HAD finally given them permission to leave the country, Pharaoh and his army were now chasing after the children of Israel furiously. After four hundred years of slavery, Moses had just begun to lead God's people joyously out of Egypt. Millions marched out with him to journey toward their own Promised Land. Now it appeared that all would be over for this bold leader Moses and all those who followed him. After all, they had an army chasing them from behind and the Red Sea right before them. All looked hopeless and impossible.

Moses began to cry to the Lord for help. The response he received, however, could make one wonder if God really cared or would intervene. "Why cry unto Me?" was the response of the Lord, who had led them into this apparent mess in the first place. I can almost see Moses as he heard this reply from God, a response that might appear at first as if to say, "Leave Me alone," or to imply "It's your problem, Moses; now you deal with it."

I am sure Moses might have initially felt somewhat like his prayers weren't going to be heard. Moses might have thought for a brief moment, "Can't God see we need Him now?"

Have you ever felt like the enemy was pursuing you from every side? Maybe you felt like there was nothing but impossibilities, just like the Red Sea that was in front of the people. Perhaps you cried to the Lord as Moses did, only to feel the same answer, "Why are you crying unto Me?" It's a feeling that God isn't listening or doesn't see the seriousness or urgency of your situation.

We all face situations like these. Whether a Red Sea or mountains and obstacles that test our walk with God, no situation or mountain is too big for God to remove. It wasn't that this mountainous situation Moses faced with the people couldn't be removed, but God was looking for something else other than a cry of desperation.

Notice the Lord's instructions in Exodus 14:15–16: "Then the LORD said to Moses, 'Why are you crying out to me? Tell the people to get moving! Pick up your staff and raise your hand over the sea. Divide the water so the Israelites can walk through the middle of the sea on dry ground'" (NLT). The Lord simply wanted Moses to know that the answer was to persistently move forward, not stand still and cry desperately. Moses must have been sure God would help them. In fact, he even told the people that God would fight for them before he began to cry to the Lord. Verse 13 says, "But Moses told the people, 'Don't be afraid. Just stand still and watch the LORD rescue you today. The Egyptians you see today will never be seen again'" (NLT). I believe the Lord wanted Moses to act on what he believed, not cry in desperate fear.

God wasn't ignoring Moses or unconcerned. Once again, God wanted to provoke a response of expectancy from Moses so that His power could move. If Moses would move forward on the earth, then God would move in heaven. Prayers must always be prayed with this type of expectancy in order to get God's attention. God wanted to intervene for Moses, but instead of a desperate cry, He was looking for Moses to step out on the words of confidence he had spoken to the people. The Lord wanted to see him act on the expectancy that God was going to move.

GO FORWARD WITH THE ROD OF POWER

We all face mountains and situations that seem impossible to remove. The problems we face sometimes seem larger than life. Just as there are different-sized mountains, we also face different-sized problems. Like with Moses, the answer to their removal doesn't come with a desperate cry. It comes by moving forward, confident in what you believe. This is because God wants us always moving forward instead of looking behind us to see what is chasing us. Moses's cry represented the fear of the enemy behind them. The Egyptians chasing them from behind reminded the people of the past, and God wanted them looking forward.

When Pharaoh pursued the people, Israel was camped out by the Red Sea. They weren't going anywhere. They were already hindered by this obstacle even before the army came after them. This is where many people live. They choose to camp out and settle for less. Instead of pressing toward the promised land, they stay in the wilderness and camp because of an obstacle or mountain. The problem is, when you camp out in the wilderness because the problem feels too big to address, the enemy will always arrive to pursue and overtake you. Instead, God wants you always moving forward.

Once God told Moses to move forward, He gave him a secret to make their progress possible. The Lord said four key words to Moses in Exodus 14:16: "Pick up your [rod]" (NLT). Could it be that Moses forgot all the wonderful things that happened when he lifted his rod in the past? The last time he lifted that rod near a body of water, it turned into blood. His rod had also become a serpent when he threw it down before the throne of Pharaoh. The very things that rod produced were what intimidated Pharaoh into letting the people go. There was authority in that rod. God wanted Moses to do just as he had done so many times before and lift up his rod of power.

We too have to lift up or stretch out our rod of authority that we have been given over the enemy—just as Moses did. Our "rod" of authority is the name of Jesus! According to Hebrews 1:1–8, Jesus holds in His hand the rod, or scepter, of righteousness. He is seated at the right hand of God with the rod of authority as Lord over everything. We are called His joint-heirs and are seated with Him in heavenly places. (See Romans 8:17; Ephesians 2:6.) That means we rule and reign with Him with that same rod of authority to overcome all the enemy has sought to do in our lives. If we call out to God and move beyond failures, memories, and pains that try to return us to bondage, then the power of the devil will be defeated by the Lord's hand.

Not only did Moses's rod of authority open a path for the people to escape, but it also completely destroyed the enemy. Look at Exodus 14:26–28: "Then the LORD said to Moses, 'Stretch out your hand over the sea so that the waters may flow back over the Egyptians and their chariots and horsemen.' Moses stretched out his hand over the sea, and at daybreak the sea went back to its place. The Egyptians were fleeing toward it, and the LORD swept them into the sea. The water flowed back and covered the chariots and horsemen—the entire army of Pharaoh that had followed the Israelites into the sea. Not one of them survived" (NIV).

We can see here that Moses's rod of authority was not only able to provide an escape route, but it also swallowed up their pursuers in the sea. When God asked why Moses was crying out to Him, it wasn't because God didn't want to be bothered or left alone. It wasn't even that

God didn't want Moses to cry out. It was because God wanted Moses to use what He had already given him. The cry that Moses offered was in fear, not in power. The Lord responded this way to get Moses to move forward rather than standing still or going backward. God wanted Moses to use his rod of power to make it possible.

We have the same "rod" of authority to move forward into our destiny regardless of the obstacles that are there to hinder us. Not only will your rod of authority open a path on dry ground, but it will also "drown" your enemies so they cannot hold you in bondage anymore.

One time my wife, her sister, and I were traveling several hours to attend a convention. The weather forecast called for snow but said it would be later on in the evening. I figured we would miss the snow by leaving in the afternoon just after work, but shortly after we started out, it began to snow very heavily. Visibility was diminishing and the wind was beginning to make the driving conditions dangerous. To make matters worse, it was getting dark and we were driving on a back highway in an attempt to save time. Some of the time we were literally out in the middle of nowhere. There was no place to stop, and the scarce hotels we passed were full. We had no choice but to keep moving slowly at about twenty-five miles per hour. It was difficult to even find a farmhouse. We were left with little option but to pray and to keep crawling forward.

While I was driving under a great deal of pressure, my sister-in-law and my wife began to pray in the spirit and speak to our mountain of seeming impossibility. We truly had no choice but to go forward, just as Moses did with the Red Sea. We finally arrived at our destination five hours beyond the normal time. But it was a perfect picture of moving forward with our rod of authority.

From that event I realized, when we face an impossible situation with little option for retreat, that with God we have the ability to move forward and lift our rod of authority to defeat the obstacles before us.

DEVELOPING A HOLY ATTITUDE OF VICTORY

The way we become confident to move forward and lift our rod of power, regardless of the mountain, is to develop a holy attitude of victory. You and I cannot be intimidated by any mountain or impossible situation. When Goliath came to intimidate Israel, David rose up with a holy attitude of victory. He just decided that this mountain was not powerful enough to overcome him. His attitude caused him to say, "Who is this uncircumcised Philistine?" (1 Samuel 17:26). His words were almost taunting of his opponent.

We too have to develop a holy attitude that says, "I will not leave You alone, God, until this mountain moves!"

We can also see a holy attitude of victory spoken by the angel to Zechariah. It was an attitude of victory that almost carried a taunting tone to it. It appeared confident and determined, saying, "Who art thou, O great mountain? before Zerubbabel thou shalt become a plain: and he shall bring forth the headstone thereof with shoutings, crying, Grace, grace unto it" (Zechariah 4:7).

That sounds like a statement with an attitude! "Who are you, O great mountain? You shall become a plain!" This needs to be your attitude too: "Who are you, mountain that stands in the way of my breakthrough? Who are you, mountain that keeps my prayer from being answered? You shall become a plain!" In other words, "I will flatten you with my attitude of faith and my words that carry power!" Rather than just accept the situation, speak to it. Jesus taught us that we can speak to the mountains in our lives and expect them to move if we believe the things we say will come to pass. (See Matthew 17:20.)

You can command grace to come to your mountainous situation. Notice the angel said, "Grace, grace unto it." What is grace? It is God's favor given to you even when you don't deserve it. I heard one man say it this way, "Grace means I *can't*, therefore God *must!*" Grace is available to deal with your mountain, and you can command grace to manifest. God wants His grace to increase and multiply on you and your situation. So expect it.

First Peter 1:2 says, "Grace unto you, and peace, be multiplied." The apostle Paul also understood this principle of moving mountains and obstacles through grace. The Bible says a messenger of Satan came to buffet Paul while he was in prison (2 Corinthians 12:7). Do you know what he did? Initially he responded like Moses and cried to the Lord to get rid of his problem. But God responded the same way He did to Moses, as if to say, "It's your deal, Paul."

So Paul cried out three times without the answer he expected from God. Finally the Lord told Paul the answer was already his. Once again, God was provoking a response so Paul could see what was already available to him. The response from God was, "My grace is sufficient for you." God wanted him to know that His grace was already there and available.

When we rise up in our authority of grace on the earth, then God will act from the grace of heaven. God's grace is sufficient for you, just as it was for Paul. Mountains will crumble from your life when you don't complain, tolerate, or go around the mountain, but instead, speak "Grace, grace" to it. And then watch it be removed. Don't leave God alone, but rise up and use what He has already given you—His rod of authority, His Word, and the name of Jesus, just to name a few. Say right now, "Who art thou, O great mountain? Right now, you become a plain! I speak grace, grace to every situation I am facing!" Grace is sufficient to level mountains and remove obstacles.

THE BURGER KING BIKER

I remember another time that I felt like I had a mountain before me in addition to a pursuing enemy behind me. It took me a minute to develop a holy attitude and see this mountain removed because at first I was intimidated.

I was driving home one evening when the Lord suddenly spoke to me to turn my car around and go back to the Burger King I had just passed. I wasn't hungry, and this wasn't where I usually stopped for a hamburger, so I began to argue with the Lord that I lived just a few blocks away and was almost home. After a few minutes of getting extremely convicted by the Lord's voice, I obeyed. I walked into the fast-food restaurant, waiting for further instruction. Oh, the instructions came all right, but not the way I wanted to receive them. I heard the Lord tell me to go into the Burger King, find the biggest man I could find, and tell him about Jesus.

I immediately disobeyed and went to a table with a small nerdy-looking boy eating a hamburger with other nerdy-looking boys. I began my evangelistic sermon only for this young man to interrupt me and point to a big biker talking in the parking lot. He said, "Why don't you tell it to that guy?" and began to laugh at me.

"Great," I thought. So God was speaking through this nerd, reminding me of my disobedience.

Finally, with great trepidation, I approached the big biker in the parking lot. He was talking to a group of people and didn't look like he wanted to be bothered. I was right; he didn't. I began to talk to him about Jesus, and he instantly began to yell at me. "Get out of here or I am going to kill you!" he said.

I didn't know what to do when he threatened to kill me, so I weakly tried to use the same line that Dave Wilkerson used in *The Cross and the Switchblade* when he witnessed to the gangs in New York. I said, "You can cut me in a million pieces if you like and try to kill me, but I will still tell you about Jesus!" His response was not so good.

"What?" he said. Then he ordered me to shut up, except this time he was clenching his fist and getting ready to hit me. He tried to punch me hard, but as his fist came toward my face, I yelled, "The blood of Jesus!" Somehow, he missed me! He repeated the effort three times, each time to no avail as I said, "The blood of Jesus!"

He and I were both surprised that not one of his punches made contact with me. This angered him even more, and he began to swing his arms while his friends tried to hold him back from me. He kept screaming and growling, "Let go; I am going to kill him!" By this time, I felt the best thing was to run, so I began to walk around to the front of the restaurant as fast as I could, but he still came after me. I heard his footsteps, and when I looked behind me, he grabbed me by my coat, picked me up, and threw me back into the front window. All I remember was hearing my mouth say, "The blood of Jesus," while my mind thought of going through the window. I looked over my shoulder as I was being thrown and saw the worker on the other side drop his mop. Somehow I bounced off the window—which I expected to go through. The biker shook his head, surprised, and became all the more angry. I shook my head too.

At this point I had had enough and got an attitude. I too was angry, but righteously angry at the demon that was driving him. Finally, I looked square at him and shouted, "I rebuke you in the name of Jesus." When I said that, demons started coming out of him! I was watching my mountain be overtaken with God's power.

By now he was visibly shaken from the anointing, so I put my hand on him and told him Jesus loved him. That night I faced what seemed like a literal Goliath, but when I quit trying to run in fear and turned to use my rod of authority, the mountain crumbled right before me. That is what God is looking for. He wants us to stand against the devil, just as I stood up to this man who tried to intimidate me. I used my rod, and the mountain fell.

PHARAOH SPIRITS OF INTIMIDATION

One of the reasons I believe Moses didn't immediately lift his rod in authority, and why the people were so afraid of their enemies, is because they needed to be delivered from the "spirit of Pharaoh." In other words, they had developed a mind-set of slavery that expected to be overcome by their captors. Think about it; that was all they knew to do for four hundred years. They knew how to be slaves. They needed to be delivered from a Pharaoh spirit.

Many of us are too intimidated to lift our rod of power because we are intimidated by the "pharaoh" that held us back for so many years. We can't see ourselves overcoming it. There are six ways a pharaoh spirit, or mind-set, will keep you from moving forward with your rod of power:

1. *It keeps you always feeling bound.* Pharaoh was a task-master, which is all about control and manipulation to keep people feeling bound and afraid.

2. *It aborts your destiny.* Pharaoh killed children in mass numbers, which represents an aborted future. He wants to abort your God-ordained future.

3. *It makes you have a small view of yourself.* All the people could see while in Egypt was that they were lesser than the Egyptians. They had a slavery mind-set and always felt like worthless victims.

4. *It will harden your heart.* Pharaoh had a hard heart and hardened it many times—even against God. The children of Israel carried that same hard-hearted rebellion out of Egypt with them.

5. *It will keep you controlled by money and possessions.* Pharaoh gave the people Goshen, which was under his control. They were always indebted there. Everything they had belonged to Pharaoh.

6. *It will try to chase and intimidate you.* Pharaoh chased the people in the wilderness, making them believe they would never be free from the past. It wants to return you to the past and intimidate you into thinking you can never overcome.

Once we expose how the spirit of Pharaoh wants to intimidate us into never seeing a breakthrough, we can begin to address it confidently with the rod of power. We need to acknowledge how that spirit covertly operates against us and then begin to speak to it in the grace of God.

At My Words

You can remove mountains when you believe it in your heart and speak to them with authority. This is what Jesus said: "If ye have faith as a grain of mustard seed, ye shall say unto this mountain, Remove hence to yonder place; and it shall remove; and nothing shall be impossible unto you" (Matthew 17:20). The best way to move a mountain from your life is to speak to it just the way Jesus taught. God told Ezekiel to prophesy to them: "Also, thou son of man, prophesy unto the mountains of Israel, and say, Ye mountains of Israel, hear the word of the LORD" (Ezekiel 36:1).

Jesus also said, "Out of the abundance of the heart the mouth speaks" (Matthew 12:34, NKJV). This means that words spoken from the heart will accomplish more than words that we say from our heads. In other words, they are words spoken from authority, right out of the depths of your heart. They are not spoken with a tone of fear attached to them.

129

Handwritten note at top: "GOD HONORS YOUR WORD - He will move on your word."

Words are powerful and can be used like a rod of authority to accomplish supernatural feats and remove mountains.

Elijah apparently understood this power in words, and he took it to another level by saying the phrase "according to *my* word." Look at what his words accomplished in 1 Kings 17:1: "As the LORD God of Israel liveth, before whom I stand, there shall not be dew nor rain these years, but according to *my word*." He was confident that his own words had enough power to affect the course of nature. That is what we find in James 3:6, which says our words can change the course of nature. For Elijah, it didn't rain because of *his* words—and God honored them.

Maybe you need some rain of trouble to stop in your life. Like the old saying goes, "When it rains, it pours." I hear so many people say that problems are just pouring over them. What rain do you need to stop with your words today? Jesus cursed a fig tree with His words, and with words He calmed the storms. You also have power in your words to change things, but you have to believe that at *your word* things will move. *Your words* are your rod of power to keep you moving forward in victory.

Some time ago I was ministering at a conference overseas where it had not rained in months, and that area was experiencing quite a drought. It was blazing hot, and you could see the effects of the lack of rain. Everywhere we went people were complaining about the heat and lack of rain.

That night as I was preaching, I was so hot and soaked with sweat while I preached. I called for the worship team to begin playing, and the prophetic anointing began to come on me. I started to prophesy to the sky and commanded the drought to stop—within twenty-four hours! I said that at *my word* it would rain as a prophetic sign to the nation that the people had elected the right leader, and God was going to show them His blessing on it through the rain. It would be a sign of answered prayer. During the prophecy the Lord also said that His voice would be heard in the heavens through the thunder.

Now there was no rain forecast, and afterward the pastors of the meeting reminded me of it. Certain pastors and leaders present in the meeting began to call other leaders across the nation, telling them I had prophesied rain as a sign. Well, the very opposite of what I had said seemed to be happening. It seemed for hours *nothing* was happening. In fact, the next day the sun seemed to mock me. I was growing very concerned about this prophetic word I had spoken.

Finally I was thrilled when later that afternoon the clouds began to form. It began to rain and rain and rain! It thundered so loudly it seemed to shake the buildings. And it rained so hard it was flooding the streets. Word traveled fast across the nation as they were seeing the drought end and God answer their prayers.

We must realize that we have the same ability as Elijah. We have power in our words if we will dare to believe. The Bible says, "Declare a thing, and it will be established for you" (Job 22:28, NKJV). Use *your* words today to decree God's will over your situation and over your life. Remember, *at your word* the power of God will move!

GO TO THE OTHER SIDE

Once again, let's review the common pattern we have seen about God throughout this book. Sometimes it seems He wants to be left alone, or doesn't respond, and it appears He is ignoring our prayers. On one occasion, in Matthew 14:22–23, Jesus even *sent* the disciples away in a boat so He could actually be alone. He asked them to cross over the water to the other side, and while Jesus was alone, they were being tossed around in the ship by a violent wind. I'm sure we can all think of times the Lord asked us to do something and it appeared that He left *us* alone, and we felt doomed to failure as if tossed out to sea. When God tells us to do something, however, He always wants us to make it to the end and cross over to the other side successfully. If it seems like He is uninvolved, perhaps He is just waiting for our response. He wants to watch us step into the power we have been given and go to the other side. In Matthew 14, when Jesus went to be alone while He sent the disciples to cross over, He wanted to test their faith and provoke a response.

When you go through tough times, it reveals a lot about who you are and what you have in you. If you were to take a sponge and put only chocolate milk in it and squeeze it, the only thing that would come out of it would be chocolate milk. What you put in you before the mountain or storm squeezes you is what will come out once pressure is applied. If you put the Word of God in you, when you are squeezed, God's Word will come out.

When Jesus sent the disciples into the storm, they panicked. The funny thing is, they had just experienced a storm on the sea a few chapters earlier in Matthew 8:23–27. Jesus rebuked them for their unbelief because somehow they still hadn't learned from the Lord's example of what to do during a storm. They didn't draw on what they had learned. First, they could have trusted Jesus's order to go successfully to the other side. Second, they should have known now how to speak to the storm, because that is how Jesus dealt with storms. Decree a thing + He shall do it.

Moses crossed to the other side with his rod of authority. Jesus also did it, and He wanted His disciples to do it. He wanted them to use their words to cross over. Proverbs 18:21 says death and life are in the *power* of the tongue. You may begin by lifting your rod of power, and it may seem like your words change the circumstance very little if at all. Our walk with God, however, is about progressive growth. The Bible says we go from revelation to revelation and from faith to faith. It is progressive. Keep lifting your rod of power to cross over, and eventually you will learn how to walk over on dry and peaceful ground.

Many years ago we faced a physical storm that reminds me of how the disciples might have felt while they were in the boat. The tornado sirens were blowing loudly and the winds had picked up drastically. My wife said the television reported a tornado was less than a mile away and heading toward our house. I couldn't see outside the back bedroom window because it was dark and raining. We stood at the window and spoke to the tornado. We commanded it to go back up in the sky *now*. Just as we said it, a huge tree branch hurled by and hit the house. Without hesitation we screamed and both ran to the basement. Forget faith for the tornado! Obviously we needed to grow in how to deal with a storm. The tornado passed by, however, and afterward we laughed and laughed at our ridiculous reaction.

Another time, a tornado rose up where we lived right next to a small medical office building. We were walking outside near the house, and the sky began to look eerie black. On our way inside, some of the doctors were outside, pointing to the sky as the cloud began to form. We walked past and said hello as they were joking about tornados destroying our homes and insurance payments and so on. We instantly told them that Jesus was going to calm this storm. Then we said we were going to speak to it. They laughed hysterically and headed in to take cover. Of course, we were heading indoors too, but first we stood and spoke to the storm. That tornado went back up in the sky and the storm began to dissipate.

Just because it looked like it worked one time for us and not another, we didn't allow that to stop us from using our rod of power to speak to the situation. Like Moses, we had no choice. We needed to stretch our voice and speak to the mountain. God's grace was available. All we had to do was use it. Those storms lifted at our words! You can be determined not to leave God alone by using what He already gave you through the power of His resurrection.

Words are a powerful force to remove mountains and calm life's storms. Whoever came up with the saying "Sticks and stones may break my bones, but words will never hurt me" was wrong! Words are more powerful than sticks and stones. The Bible says words go into a man's heart and soul. I have listed some other things the Bible says about the power of our words:

- Words are to be acceptable in God's sight (Psalm 19:14).
- We are snared by our words (Proverbs 6:2).
- Our words should be excellent and righteous (Proverbs 8:6–9).
- We will be satisfied with good by words, and health will be the result (Proverbs 12:14, 18).
- Good words make our hearts glad (Proverbs 12:25).

Do you know that words can hurt and cause people to carry ill effects from them for a lifetime? When God created the universe, He did it with words. All creation exists because of words, and it is still being held together by the *word* of His power (Hebrews 1:3). Words were used in the Bible to speak to storms, mountains, fig trees, demons, and the heavens. We must train our tongue to speak what God says about our mountains or situations in our lives, for it is the rod of power. When you make a habit of speaking God's Word, you will see mountains move. Don't leave God alone by choosing to speak the right words. We must keep our tongue from speaking evil and negative things. In times of trouble, we need to be careful not to speak out of fear and frustration, but speak to our mountains with words of victory and faith.

SEVEN BLESSINGS OF OBEYING AND SPEAKING GOD'S WORD

Your words can get you through your most difficult times and mountainous situations. Don't leave God alone by continually speaking His Word from your mouth. This is how you learn to be obedient to God's Word, by constantly speaking it. It is that obedience to His Word that will cause you to enter your land of promise. Israel experienced seven blessings from speaking and then obeying God's Word. They are found in Leviticus 26:3–13.

134

1. *You will have God's open heaven of increase.* "Then I will give you rain in due season, and the land shall yield her increase, and the trees of the field shall yield their fruit" (verse 4).

2. *You will have an overflow of blessings.* "And your threshing shall reach unto the vintage, and the vintage shall reach unto the sowing time: and ye shall eat your bread to the full, and dwell in your land safely" (verse 5).

3. *You will have peace and protection and will dwell in safety.* "And I will give peace in the land, and ye shall lie down, and none shall make you afraid: and I will rid evil beasts out of the land, neither shall the sword go through your land" (verse 6).

4. *You will be delivered from your enemies.* "And ye shall chase your enemies, and they shall fall before you by the sword. And five of you shall chase an hundred, and an hundred of you shall put ten thousand to flight: and your enemies shall fall before you by the sword" (verses 7–8).

5. *You will enjoy the multiplied blessings of your covenant.* "For I will have respect unto you, and make you fruitful, and multiply you, and establish my covenant with you" (verse 9).

6. *You will experience a new harvest.* "And ye shall eat old store, and bring forth the old because of the new" (verse 10).

7. *The Lord's presence will be with you.* "And I will walk among you, and will be your God, and ye shall be my

people. I am the LORD your God, which brought you forth out of the land of Egypt, that ye should not be their bondmen; and I have broken the bands of your yoke, and made you go upright" (verses 12–13).

All of these promises are yours if you will take your eyes off your past and put them on your future with the Lord. Go boldly forward with God's rod of authority in your mouth. Remember the pursuing army of Pharaoh was Israel's past, and the Red Sea had to be crossed with authority for them to enter their future blessings. Impossible as it would seem that a sea could part in two, all things are possible with God. What may seem impossible for us is not impossible for Him. We don't need to cry out in unbelief or fear. We can stretch our rod of authority—God's Word of promise in our mouths—and go straightforward. "Who art thou, O great mountain or storm? You are a plain today!"

Let me encourage you, don't leave God alone. Be encouraged to go forward with your rod of power and not leave Him alone until every mountain has been completely taken out of your way!

8

I WILL NOT LEAVE YOU ALONE UNTIL DEAD DREAMS COME TO LIFE AGAIN

Now a certain man named Lazarus was ill. He was of Bethany, the village where Mary and her sister Martha lived. This Mary was the one who anointed the Lord with perfume and wiped His feet with her hair. It was her brother Lazarus who was [now] sick. So the sisters sent to Him, saying, Lord, he whom You love [so well] is sick. When Jesus received the message, He said, This sickness is not to end in death; but [on the contrary] it is to honor God and to promote His glory, that the Son of God may be glorified through (by) it. Now Jesus loved Martha and her sister and Lazarus. [They were His dear friends, and He held them in loving esteem.] Therefore [even] when He heard that Lazarus was sick, He still stayed two days longer in the same place where He was.

—John 11:1–6, AMP

TWO MORE DAYS! What could Jesus be thinking? This was not some stranger, but it was Lazarus, His friend, who was dying. If there was ever a time to hurry and visit him, this was it. Perhaps Jesus didn't realize the seriousness of the situation at hand when the message came to Him. I'm sure there were a number of things going through the minds of Mary, Martha, and Jesus's disciples when the news of Lazarus was received. Yet Jesus didn't respond as they expected, or even the way they wanted Him to respond.

According to Scripture, when He heard that Lazarus was sick, He deliberately waited two more days before paying His sick friend a visit. Was this another example of God wanting to be alone or ignoring a request? It seemed as if Jesus was not going to do anything. He had healed so many before; why not run quickly to His dear friend?

We know for sure that Mary and Martha *were* offended that He seemingly ignored their desperate message. In fact, the Bible says that by the time Jesus finally arrived, Lazarus had been dead four days! So the minute Martha saw Jesus, her offense came out, and she confronted Jesus with, "Lord, if You had been here, my brother would not have died" (John 11:21, NKJV).

Wow! What a hello greeting. She was angry and let Jesus know about it. In other words, she was saying, "Jesus, if You wouldn't have ignored our urgent prayer and came when we asked, our brother would not be dead today." Her attitude prevented her from seeing the miracle that was about to occur. Look at verse 39: "Jesus said, 'Take away the stone.' Martha, the sister of him who was dead, said to Him, 'Lord, by this time there is a stench, for he has been dead four days'" (NKJV). Even though the stone was being rolled away, she could only see the negative.

Then what about her sister Mary? She was sitting in her house most assuredly grieving and also offended that the Lord didn't come. John 11:20 says, "But Mary sat still in the house." She went on to speak her mind in verse 32: "Lord, if thou hadst been here, my brother had not died." She said the exact same thing as her sister Martha. That wasn't an accident. They probably talked about their feelings before, and now they were mad. Jesus was considered a friend of the family, and that fact only added to why they were offended when He didn't come in their moment of need.

When you are desperate, you expect your friends to be there for you, right? Jesus went for others who were in need, so why not His close friends? They had a dream in their heart that Jesus would come and rescue Lazarus so that he wouldn't die. They had a dream that their brother would always be a part of their lives. But now that dream had died and Jesus didn't do anything to stop it.

Of course, Jesus never does anything without a purpose. Instead, He had a purpose, to provoke a response, to see what they were going to do. He was looking for a response of faith, but instead they became offended when He didn't do what was expected. The only thing He told them was that this situation would lead to God being glorified. How could that happen? Lazarus was dead!

While they saw a dead dream, however, Jesus was seeing a dead dream about to be resurrected. He wanted Mary and Martha to respond with an attitude that they weren't going to quit believing or give up—that they weren't going to leave God alone about it, even though it looked hopeless. Jesus wanted them to respond in faith that, even though their dream had died, not all was lost, but their dead dream was going to come to life again.

THE RESURRECTION OF OUR LAZARUS

Have you ever had something urgent that you needed God to answer, and it felt like you had to have it right now? Did it seem as if your answer didn't come the way you expected or in the time frame you needed? Perhaps your dreams about the future seem to be dying right before your eyes. Several years ago, we had a Lazarus situation like that in our family. It was our own dream that was dying, and it appeared the Lord was not intervening. At first, it seemed God was not answering our prayers, and it felt at times like He wasn't listening. Yet, we kept believing that our dream would come to pass. Our family learned the importance of not leaving God alone until our dead dream came back to life.

It really started on July 4 during a family camping trip, when my wife's father came down with a very high fever of 104 degrees. The cause of the fever went undiagnosed by several doctors as antibiotics brought the fever under control after three weeks. He seemed to recover, but he remained weak for some time. By the first week of December, the high and mysterious fever came back with a fury. He woke up one morning, faint and seeing spots. So my mother-in-law called for an ambulance.

It turned out that his situation was so serious they decided to move him by helicopter to another medical facility, thinking at first it was his heart. Emergency exploratory surgery, however, found he had diverticulitis and his bowel had ruptured. His infection was so bad that he went into septic shock from months of having an undetected, ruptured bowel. Now, in just a few hours, he was near death. If he had gone back to bed that morning, he would have been dead when my mother-in-law returned home from work that evening.

While surgery repaired the bowel, his body was so poisoned that he had to be placed in a medical coma to attempt some sort of recovery. He immediately swelled to three times his normal size, his fever went to 105 degrees, and there were nineteen intravenous bags of medicines, fluids, blood, and food hanging over his head. He had eight physicians on his case. His liver, kidneys, and lungs all began shutting down because of the infection. He was placed on full dialysis and a ventilator, experiencing what is known as multiple organ and renal failure.

My wife and her sister drove to see their dad. Little did we know that we were all about to enter one of the greatest spiritual battles of our lives. We were in prayer literally around the clock. I was at home about three hours away caring for our two small children, one of them only an infant. The first report from the surgeon was that there was less than a 50 percent chance of his survival. My mother-in-law calmly but firmly said, "Doctor, my God is bigger than that. I believe we should stay on the 50 percent side of the positive then!"

After seven days, I drove there with our children. When our oldest son, just in grade school at the time, saw his grandpa, he said, "Grandpa, you take up your bed and go home praising God!"

At first, our dream felt like it was dying as days went by with little change in our dad's condition. Sometimes it felt like our prayers weren't working. After two weeks went by, however, Dad still hadn't died. Of course, he wasn't being declared better by doctors, but he certainly wasn't dead. He had lived longer than expected. Something must have been happening. Sometimes when we are in a trial, we can't see the miracle slowly taking place.

Mary and Martha never noticed that a miracle was about to occur when Jesus took away the stone from Lazarus's grave. Removing the stone should have been a loud message to them that a miracle was on the way. For us, the Lord began to give us all many different signs to show us He was rolling away the stone. We would have a little vision here, and a dream or a scripture there. This was the Lord rolling back our stone, trying to prepare us to receive a miracle. We held on to everything the Lord gave us, waiting for our Lazarus to rise up. We refused to leave God alone until our dead dream came to life again.

One day my wife, Brenda, prayed and said, "Lord, let the doctors call him 'miracle man.'" One doctor heard, and before long all of them began to talk more positively and started calling him "miracle man." Then slowly he began having a miracle recovery.

Little by little his medicines were reduced, machines were removed, and then one day he woke up. The staff who worked there were overjoyed to see him. When he was finally moved from the ICU, one nurse who hadn't seen him in a while put her hand over her mouth in disbelief and said, "Oh my God! That's the man from room ten." Later his surgeon said, "It certainly wasn't anything we physicians did. It was a work of faith and prayer." They say most people don't normally survive septic shock, but now it has been several years since this event, and all is well with God's "miracle man."

I am telling you things will happen when you refuse to leave God alone about the dreams in your life. What is important to you? Unlike Mary and Martha, expect your dream to live today, and don't allow the stone to be rolled away while you are crying in unbelief. See your dead dream alive and well, and stay after it until it comes to pass!

OVERCOMING PITFALLS TO YOUR DREAMS

In every dream that we have in life, the enemy has set pitfalls to keep our dream bound in the grave like Lazarus. You have a choice to give up because of them or to keep plowing through. Jesus walked past every possible pitfall after He received the news of Lazarus. From John 11, I want to uncover the pitfalls that the devil uses to keep you from fulfilling your dreams in life.

Pitfall 1: Bad news

"Lord, your dear friend is very sick" (verse 3, NLT). It is important when pursuing your dream not to react to bad or negative news that sometimes comes to you. Just because something doesn't work out at first doesn't mean it won't work out later. The way to avoid the pitfall of bad news is to speak to the situation. "When Jesus heard that, He said, 'This sickness is not unto death, but for the glory of God'" (verse 4, NKJV). He took a negative situation and spoke victory.

Pitfall 2: Wrong timing

"Now Jesus loved Martha, and her sister, and Lazarus. When he heard therefore that he was sick, he abode two days still" (verses 5–6). Jesus said He only did that which His Father told Him and followed God's timing instead of His own. He loved this family and probably wanted to be there for them, but He realized the important thing was to be led by the Spirit. Don't respond out of fear even though it is tempting to react to the situation rather than, like Jesus, be led by the Spirit of God and remain in faith.

Pitfall 3: Friends and family

"His disciples say unto him..." (verse 8). When the disciples heard that Lazarus was sick and Jesus was delaying His response, they began to offer their opinions. Friends and family can be sincere, but sometimes sincerely wrong. Job's friends were his greatest critics and gave him wrong advice. Those close to us can often be a help, but they can also hinder our dreams through too much familiarity with us and with our situation. Even Jesus could not perform His greatest miracles in His hometown because of people who knew Him so well that they could not see His spiritual purpose. (See Mark 6:1–4.)

Pitfall 4: Fear and worry

"The Jews sought to stone You, and are You going there again?" (John 11:8, NKJV). Fear is one of the greatest things the devil uses to keep your dream dead in the grave like Lazarus. Jesus had previously been attacked in Judea when people wanted to stone Him. Instead of allowing fear to render Him ineffective or cause Him to adjust His plans, Jesus didn't let fear immobilize Him. Fears can be thoughts we form in our mind that convince us not to embrace our future hopes and dreams.

Pitfall 5: The past

"Are You going there again?" (verse 8, NKJV). To raise Lazarus from the dead, Jesus was going to have to face a past occurrence and go to Judea again. He didn't let a past experience keep Him from a future miracle. It is important to not live in the past or revert back to it while forming your decisions. We need to face the future with victory. Many people relate to their future from their past experiences. If they have failed in the past, they think they will fail in the future. Don't let past mistakes, fears, and failures keep you from trying again.

Pitfall 6: Unbelief

"Then said Thomas...Let us also go, that we may die with him" (verse 16). Thomas was convinced that Jesus was setting them up to fail. And unbelief is the very thing that will set you up to fail. It was unbelief that kept the children of Israel from entering into their Promised Land. We are often like Thomas, without vision, faith, or a positive outlook about where the Lord leads. Unbelief doesn't let you see the promise of your dream. Instead it makes you see the impossibility of it.

Pitfall 7: Impossible situations

"Then when Jesus came, he found that he had lain in the grave four days already" (verse 17). Lazarus had already been dead for four days. Jewish custom believed that after three days, there was no possible hope of anyone returning from the dead. Jesus waited on purpose to show that He had power over death by raising a man who had been dead four days and to show a picture of His own coming resurrection. Perhaps you have a situation that looks hopeless to you—with little or no possibilities. Lazarus coming back to life gives us hope that our dead dreams can come back to life even when it doesn't look remotely possible. We serve a God of impossibilities!

Pitfall 8: Apathy

"Then Martha, as soon as she heard that Jesus was coming, went and met him: but Mary sat still in the house" (verse 20). Mary was sitting in her house most assuredly upset because Jesus seemed to be ignoring her request to come to her brother's aid. It would seem she quit caring because she didn't come right out to see Jesus when He arrived. We have a choice to either continue to pursue God even when we don't understand what is happening or, like Mary, give up and stop pursuing the hope of our dream being raised. When it looks like the Lord is not listening to our dreams, or situations aren't looking like we want them to, then it is time to get out of the "house mentality" and start seeking the Lord where He can be found.

Pitfall 9: Excuses and blame

"If You had been here, my brother would not have died" (verse 32, NKJV). It was obvious Mary was placing the responsibility for Lazarus's death on Jesus. She felt He should have done something to keep it from happening. So she resorted to blaming Him for not being there earlier. It is always easy to point the finger at someone or something else when it seems our desires are not working out. Sometimes we use excuses to justify our position. Mary could have refused to leave God alone by believing He was going to help her dreams stay alive. Instead, she blamed the Lord and excused her own behavior.

Pitfall 10: Wrong emotions

"Jesus saw her weeping, and the Jews who came with her weeping..." (verse 33, NKJV). It is OK to cry, but not to stay in a state of despair. The Jews, in their custom, would often cry and mourn as part of tradition. It was soulish and produced nothing. We are to be led by the Spirit instead of our emotions. If we spend too long weeping, we can progress into unbelief and open ourselves to the spirit of grief. I know people today who still cry over a situation from long ago, but there comes a point where wrong emotions will keep our future dreams in the grave. We need to align our emotions with God and His plans for our future.

Pitfall 11: Religion and tradition

"Could not this man, which opened the eyes of the blind, have caused that even this man should not have died?" (verse 37). Those who came to the tomb of Lazarus began to bring an accusation against the Lord. They began casting doubt that Jesus could raise Lazarus, probably because their tradition doubted His power. Religion uses human reason to try to explain supernatural experiences, and it reduces them to nothing more than a common occurrence. Religious spirits were the only spirits that didn't bow to Jesus—they crucified Him and resisted Him. Human reasoning will limit you and talk you out of your dream coming to life.

Pitfall 12: Obstacles and resistance

"Take away the stone" (verse 39, NKJV). The stone on the tomb of Lazarus represented an obstacle between Mary and Martha and their dream. We can't be discouraged by resistance to our faith. There may be a stone between us and our dreams, but we have to be persistent until it moves out of the way. Many dreams have been left in the grave because people didn't want to deal with the obstacles in front of them. So they chose to give up and shift their focus elsewhere. God is waiting for us to remove the stones and obstacles resisting us so He can bring our dream forth.

Satan always puts these twelve pitfalls in our paths in order to keep our dreams and desires in a cave, where they are confined with no signs of life. Jesus overcame these barriers so you can be positioned to raise your dreams and have your prayers answered. Once you become aware of the pitfalls to your dreams, you will find yourself ready to bring your dead dreams to life again.

By Now It Stinks

When Jesus arrived to see Mary, Martha, and the family, He asked them a normal question that carried a prophetic significance. In John 11:34, He said, "Where have you laid him?" (NKJV). In other words, He was asking, "Where is your dream? What has become of it?"

Your answer to that question might be the same as Martha's in John 11:39, when she said, "Lord, by this time he stinketh." Like her, you might be saying, "It is in a cave, Lord, and by now it stinks. I haven't been able to do anything with it, and by now it has become stale!" That is exactly what they said about Lazarus who had been dead four days. The stench of a dead dream was all they could see.

To make a good comparison, think of something you remember smelling that was really bad. Maybe it was the trash or something you found forgotten in your refrigerator. Recall something that smelled totally repulsive.

I understand the meaning of "by now it stinks!" Before I got married, I had a roommate who brought home a huge bowl of taco salad that his girlfriend had made on Thanksgiving weekend. We ate some of it and stored the leftovers in the oven because the bowl didn't fit in our refrigerator. Yes, you can only imagine. Of course, we forgot about it because we couldn't cook and never used the oven. Months later, we smelled a rotten smell somewhere in our kitchen. Then our noses led us back to the oven. It was horrible! Not knowing what to do with the contaminated, oversized Tupperware bowl of rotted matter, my roommate threw the thing outside on the back porch. The problem was, true to bachelor living, we forgot about it again until spring. Then from the window, the evil smell made its way back into the house. It was the worst smell I can ever remember. I tell you, it stunk! It wasn't even salad now. It was some sort of biology project of horror. It smelled like something really big had died.

This is where many Christians are when it comes to their dreams. "By now it stinks" were the words Martha spoke to describe her feelings about her brother's death. The truth of the matter is that we would all probably have said the same thing if we would have been there. We tend to see the negative—we see and smell the stink. It looks so badly rotted that it looks hopeless to raise it back to life again.

We are often like Martha in that we can't have faith for the future that an impossible situation can change. Perhaps the dream you desire is to be free from an addiction or be healed from a disease or some other prayer that is yet to be answered. Maybe it appears the situation you are facing stinks and smells of dead dreams and hopes. You must always remember that God sees life in the middle of dead situations. He speaks healing instead of sickness, success rather than failure. We can become easily discouraged because we often tend to think that too much time has passed for our dream to be raised up again.

When I was first trying to find my way into ministry, I felt many times like my dreams were dying and rotting. I will never forget the words I heard the Lord say as I was driving one afternoon. "Hank," He said, "for the next seven years you will be like Joseph. You will be falsely accused and hated by some." Those words from the Lord were so shocking that I pulled over to the side of the road and cried. Little did I know that it would lead to me being fired twice in a year. The first time was from a ministry position and the second time from secular work.

When I was fired the first time from ministry, I was a young husband and father, and it caused me to have to sell my first house. It forced me to move with no money and no place to live, but still hearing the words scream in my ears concerning ministry: "You will be like Joseph the next seven years."

I remember how my wife and I felt in that season. I felt confused in my heart, feeling like God was angry and mad at me for some reason. Feeling empty and like God had forgotten me, I spent those years trying to find my way back into ministry. I couldn't figure out why my circumstances were so opposite of all God told us, and even what countless others had prophesied about our future. I didn't know that before our dream of ministry could arise, we had to go through a process and remove some obstacles. I just felt God was ignoring me on purpose. "What did I do to deserve all of this?" I thought.

Then seven years later, the Lord spoke again, this time in a way that seemed almost audible to me. "Hank, will you pastor? Go to Omaha and start a church for Me." I could hardly believe my ears. After all the turmoil, hurt, and not leaving God alone in the midst of our dreams, He was now speaking to us to start a church. I talked it over with my pastor, and that was the beginning of the resurrection of our dreams.

I learned some things during that time. I really felt like Joseph, who had a dream, told it to his brothers, and was thrown into a pit, then a prison, and later promoted to the palace. I realized it is important to hold on to your dream and be careful with whom you share it. For Joseph, God put in his path three people who represented three types of people God will use to point us toward our dreams. For Joseph it was the baker, the butler, and Pharaoh. We will also encounter a "baker," a "butler," and a "Pharaoh." Here is what they represent for us:

- *The baker:* These are the people whom God puts in your life to bring all the ingredients together. They help you fulfill your dreams by supplying resources and places for your dream to rise and grow.

- *The butler:* The butlers in your life are those whom God divinely connects you with by way of relationships that will open doors of opportunity for you to serve in your dream.

- *Pharaoh:* The pharaohs that the Lord will align you with are those who will help create a position for your dream and use your skills and talents to be a blessing to others.

All three of these helped aid Joseph to his dream and will be keys for your dreams as well. It seemed like God had forgotten about Joseph and left him in a pit and in prison. He allowed him to be falsely accused. In the end we see that the Lord didn't forget about him, but He was working to promote Joseph and fulfill his dream. I realized later in my life that God was doing the same with us. We held on to the Lord and sought Him, and eventually our dream for ministry came to life.

When Jesus stood at the grave of Lazarus, He spoke three commands that teach ways of not leaving God alone until our Lazarus situations are raised. The three commands He gave were, "Take away the stone," "Lazarus, come forth," and "Loose him and let him go." All are significant actions to follow for your dream to be raised.

REMOVE THE STONE!

The first command was, "Take away the stone" (John 11:39, NKJV). Notice Jesus didn't remove the stone, but He expected someone else to do it. First, the Lord wants us to remove our obstacles, not always wait for Him to do something. We must take responsibility to remove the stones in our lives that are keeping us from living in new life and walking with God. Secondly, it is a call for us to do things we have never done before. Why does He expect us to remove the stone or do something we have never done? So He can move us into the miraculous that lies on the other side.

God wants every person to take away the stone because the result will be supernatural blessings. Mary and Martha were only one stone away from a miracle. In the same way, there may be only one stone keeping you from your dream or answered prayer. Jesus will not remove the stone; He wants us to do it. That is another example of what it really means to not leave God alone. Begin removing obstacles obstructing your contact with the anointing.

Many times we wait for something or someone else to remove the obstacles that we are facing. But look at John 11:41. It says, "Then *they* took away the stone from the place where the dead was laid" (emphasis added). Who took away the stone? *They* took away the stone. Someone had to rise up and decide to do it.

If we want those things that are keeping our blessings from us to be removed, then we have to do the same. It was their responsibility to make the way for Jesus to move. The reason the Lord is not able to move in many people's lives is because they are not removing the stones that are preventing them.

Some of the stones we need to remove are the ones we allow to harden our hearts to the Lord and His Word. If those who witnessed a miracle that day would have chosen to be spectators rather than participants in removing the stone, there would have been no supernatural manifestation.

We must learn to take what is ours. We have a right to be free and have our prayers answered, but it means we have to do something. Numbers 32:5–6 says, "Wherefore, said they, if we have found grace in thy sight, let this land be given unto thy servants for a possession, and bring us not over Jordan. And Moses said unto the children of Gad and to the children of Reuben, Shall your brethren go to war, and shall ye sit here?" We can see from this verse that some refuse to take what is theirs. They want to sit while others do the work for them. The children of Gad and Reuben had a land promised to them, but they wanted to settle for less because they didn't want to fight for it.

Let me encourage you to rise up and remove whatever hindrance is telling you that you will never rise again or that what you are praying for will never come to pass. The Lord is waiting for our obedience to do what He says. It starts with not leaving God alone until we see our prayers and dreams brought to manifestation. Jesus performed this miracle in a place called *Bethany*, which means "the house of unripe figs" or "the house of misery." In other words, it was a place where there was no fruit coming to manifestation. The raising of Lazarus occurred in Bethany, right in the place of misery.

If you remove your obstacles, even in the midst of misery and fruitlessness, your dream will rise up. For Mary and Martha, Lazarus was the fruit that came to life and, ultimately, touched the whole city, causing many to believe. For them, Bethany was no longer a house of unripe figs or misery. It became a new place where dead dreams came back to life.

Telling Your Dream to Come Forth

The second command Jesus gave was, "Lazarus, come forth" (John 11:43). The Lord wants our prayers to be answered and our dreams fulfilled. He wants them to come out of the grave. Our dreams coming alive do not just affect us but others as well. Jesus said Lazarus would be raised in order to glorify God. All of Lazarus's family would experience the power of God when one dead man came back to life. The raising up of this man created quite a stir, but it caused many to believe on Jesus. We see it in John 12:10–11, "But the chief priests consulted that they might put Lazarus also to death; Because that by reason of him many of the Jews went away, and believed on Jesus."

God wants us to be determined about our dreams coming out of the grave so many others will be blessed by our miracle. Just as it was with Jesus, the key is that you will have to command it to live. You have to call it out of the grave. When you do, it may not appear immediately, but be assured it will come forth.

Before our prayers, desires, or dreams are brought forth, it may feel like a period of delay. Mary and Martha experienced delay when Jesus waited or delayed His arrival by two days. It appeared the dream or request wouldn't be answered. God used a delay to see if they were determined to bring their dreams out of the grave. This delay ultimately sent a message to the spirits of death, hell, and the grave that they would no longer hold the keys because, just as Lazarus rose, so would Jesus rise. Delay could not keep a dream from coming forth.

There are also demonic delays. When Daniel prayed, his prayers were delayed for twenty-one days. (See Daniel 10:13.) Then God sent His angel Michael to tell him that the first day he prayed, his prayers were heard in heaven. A spirit called the prince of Persia, however, had delayed the answer.

When we pray according to Revelation 8, the angels take our prayers before the throne of God, and they are brought back to us as answers in the earth. Many times when our prayers or dreams are delayed, it isn't that God isn't answering, but rather they are being delayed by evil spirits. These spirits stand as stones or barriers to keep what we desire from manifesting. Then we have to command our dreams to come forth or to live by using our authority over these spirits. We have authority over them to bind their influence and see our answers come.

A third kind of delay is due to our own choices in which the Holy Ghost must help us get back on course with God. Joseph had a dream that was delayed by his own unwise choice to share it proudly with others in his family. This led to a delay in his dream and God working a refreshed course for him to take. His decision now included the pit, the prison, and finally the throne. It may have seemed God wasn't answering Joseph and had forgotten him, but this wasn't the case. God was reworking a path for Joseph to follow because of his own choices. Overcoming this kind of delay requires the ingredients of faith and patience. Faith unlocks the doors and gets God's attention, while patience demonstrates that, no matter what it looks like along the way, we expect our dreams to come forth.

Remember, Jesus's crying for Lazarus to come forth wasn't just a cry for a friend to come to life. It was rather a cry of victory over death that brought revival—meaning "life again" to dead situations and dreams. You should tell your dream to come forth every day. Wake up and expect to see it walking toward you. At times, there may be delays, but don't let them stop you from telling your dream to come out of the grave.

LOOSE AND LET GO

"Loose him, and let him go" (John 11:44). That was Jesus's third command. Even though Lazarus walked out of the grave, he was still wearing graveclothes. He was free to experience a new life, but still wearing graveclothes that bound his head, his hands, and his feet. The first part of verse 44 says, "And he that was dead came forth, bound hand and foot with graveclothes: and his face was bound about with a napkin."

We are often the same way with our dream. Even though it has been resurrected, we still have a grave mind-set. We live in the present as we once lived in the past. We respond to things as we did before our dreams came to life. These "graveclothes," or habits, need to be removed just as Jesus commanded they be removed from Lazarus. Lazarus was bound in three places, which represents the three mind-sets, or prisons, we stay in even though we are living our dream.

1. *Bound hands:* This is anything that limits or hinders you from serving, laboring, and working your ministry. It is hard to accomplish anything when something is restricting your efforts.

2. *Bound feet:* This would be things that make you fall. They are habits and sins from the past coming back to haunt you so that you never really walk forward successfully.

3. *Bound face:* These graveclothes were on Lazarus's head, eyes, mouth, and ears. They hindered vision, speech, hearing, and thoughts. Your dream may be manifest, but you cannot seem to grasp the blessing of it in order to move on. Each part of the face is restricted by these graveclothes.

   - Eyes—no vision, direction, or new purpose for the future
   - Mouth—no ability to speak and decree the Word of the Lord

- Ears—no hearing for God's fresh rhema Word, but only hearing the negative
- Thoughts—no ability to think according to a renewed mind; instead, you think according to your past life, failures, and mistakes.

Once we step into the dream God gave us, we need to "loose it, and let it go." Our destiny doesn't end with the dream coming out of the grave—it has only begun. We can't hang around the tomb, rejoicing about our breakthrough but unable to walk on from there because of graveclothes. The devil will use spirits or "graveclothes" to bind you so your dream is alive but limited.

When Jezebel died, only her skull, hands, and feet remained (2 Kings 9:35). Jezebel speaks of bondage and the places left in our lives that are still being bound. What remained of her were the same places where Lazarus wore the graveclothes that bound him (John 11:44). Have you noticed how Jesus was pierced in the same places—His head, hands, and feet? Just as the remains of Jezebel spoke of bondage, now, on Jesus, they spoke of freedom.

We don't have to be controlled by a Jezebel spirit and bound by the graveclothes. It is time for you to be "loosed and let go" so you can enjoy living in your dream and move to the next place God has for you.

Like Mary and Martha, you can have dead dreams and unanswered prayers come to life. You may have some dead dreams that don't seem like they are ever going to work out. Maybe it's dead desires or hopes—and by now they are stinking. Don't get offended and give up or start blaming the Lord for why something didn't happen the way you expected. Keep believing for your dream and refuse to leave God alone, and you will eventually see your own dead dreams come to life!

9

I WILL NOT LEAVE YOU ALONE UNTIL I CHANGE

And they came to Jericho: and as he went out of Jericho with his disciples and a great number of people, blind Bartimaeus, the son of Timaeus, sat by the highway side begging. And when he heard that it was Jesus of Nazareth, he began to cry out, and say, Jesus, thou son of David, have mercy on me.

—Mark 10:46–47

JESUS, THOU SON of David, have mercy upon me!" A man, a blind beggar named Bartimaeus, cried out to the Lord as He was leaving the town of Jericho. This could be his only chance to change. He had to make sure that he would be heard in order to get the attention of Jesus. He cried with everything he had, only to have the crowd quiet him down. He just wasn't going to allow anything to stop him, so he cried all the more.

At first his cries seemed to be ignored or unheard by the Lord. It looked as though he would have to live another day in his condition without any help or change. He was all alone and looked down on by some who didn't understand his desperate need. Little did he know that his moment of transformation was about to come. His persistent request stopped Jesus in His tracks, and this insignificant man named Bartimaeus was forever changed.

The story of blind Bartimaeus teaches us the important principle of how to press into the Lord until change comes to our lives. His deep heart cry was, "I will not leave You alone until I change." Jesus stood still because one person persisted in trying to get His attention and wouldn't leave Him alone. There are several ways Bartimaeus sought the change he so desperately needed. We can step into the same level of miraculous change if we follow his example.

He refused to leave Jesus alone.

Mark 10:47 says, "And when he heard that it was Jesus of Nazareth, he began to cry out, and say, Jesus, thou son of David, have mercy on me." It was Bartimaeus's determination to keep reaching and calling for Jesus, even though he was blind and lived every day in unchanged darkness. The more he felt hindered by the crowd or unnoticed by the Lord, the louder and bolder he became. Because he was blind, he wasn't able to discern how close he was to his answer. He just persistently called out.

In the same way we often don't discern how close we are to being changed and that our breakthrough is within our reach. His cry was with a feeling of abandonment. It was similar to Jesus's cry on the cross when He said, "My God, My God why hast thou forsaken me?" (Matthew 27:46). We often think the same way, feeling that no one knows the depth of darkness we are experiencing. It could be compared to a lost child who can't find his parents in a store.

The first time Bartimaeus "cried" out for Jesus, he spoke the Greek word *boao* (Luke 18:38), meaning to shout or cry out. It is a strong word indicating to cry out deeply and loudly. And when more people tried to make him be quiet, he "cried" so much more, *krazo* (verse 39), which is an entirely different Greek word. It means to take the cry to the next level of intensity and even make a scene. He had to yell louder now because he had to be heard over the crowd telling him to be quiet. He refused to accept that. This is important because it reveals how he made a decision to not let others, or even himself, keep him from being changed in the Lord's presence. Initially he cried out loudly, but when he realized his moment of change might get away from him, he used a different cry. It was a cry that got the Lord's attention.

He truly wanted to change.

Mark 10:51 says, "And Jesus answered and said unto him, What wilt thou that I should do unto thee? The blind man said unto him, Lord, that I might receive my sight." Bartimaeus didn't hesitate to tell Jesus what he wanted—he wanted to change; he wanted to see. He was tired of walking in darkness and stumbling through life. This is important because, until we determine that we want to change, we often won't. You have to be determined to change and be dissatisfied with your current lifestyle or condition.

He was specific about what he wanted changed.

Jesus asked Bartimaeus what he wanted. His response to the Lord in verse 51 was specific when he said, "I want to receive my sight." When you are specific about what areas you really want to change, it shows the difference between a heart choice and a head choice. By the level of Bartimaeus's cry, it revealed the depth of the desire he had for his heart to change. When you are not specific about what change you want, then it hasn't yet become a heart decision that will bring satisfying results.

He wanted change now.

Mark 10:46 says, "And they came to Jericho: and as he went out of Jericho with his disciples and a great number of people, blind Bartimaeus, the son of Timaeus, sat by the highway side begging." Jesus was leaving Jericho, and it was now or perhaps never for this blind beggar Bartimaeus. Jesus was going a different direction, and Bartimaeus had to determine that now—not later—was the only way to seize his moment. He could have used any excuse to not grab hold of this moment. Many stay in the same manner of lifestyle, unchanged because they feel everything has to be perfect—including themselves—before change can happen in their lives.

He didn't let others stop him from his day of change.

Mark 10:48 says, "And many charged him that he should hold his peace: but he cried the more a great deal, Thou son of David, have mercy on me." If Bartimaeus was going to seize his moment and have his life forever changed by the Lord, he could not be bothered by what others were saying. Oftentimes the devil will use others, or even demonic spirits, to tell us that it's no use, to just stop praying, or not to expect a change. Bartimaeus wanted to change, and others tried to make him feel that it wasn't his day for it. True conversion comes in your life when you are determined to change—and it is not based on the feelings of anyone else. Only you can initiate the change that brings you from darkness to light.

He let go of his own security.

Mark 10:50 says, "And he, casting away his garment, rose, and came to Jesus." The garment of this blind beggar was the covering of a blind man. It had been used for many things, like keeping him warm, and was spread out so passersby could place money on it. Throwing aside his garment revealed that he was ready to let go of his "security blanket" or familiar garment. It paints us a picture of coming out of our comfort zone and becoming totally dependent on the new life the Lord gives.

When it comes to change, it can be instant or it can occur progressively over time as we make decisions to become different every day. Jesus took a man named Simon, whose name meant "to bend in the wind like a reed," and converted him into Peter, which means "the rock." Peter had to go through a series of things that brought him from one who was like a reed just blowing and bending in man's direction to a stable rock who later became a mighty apostle of the Lord.

The Bible says we are changed into His image. Change is not always easy, nor is it necessarily enjoyable. When we are serious about changing and we become more like Christ, as Bartimaeus did, we may have those who try to discourage us. But we can't bend toward their influence. When Bartimaeus was crying out, the crowd tried to influence him to be quiet. It is important to watch out for people and things that will tell you to be quiet or back away from God in your most desperate time of need. There are always those who will try to discourage your radical cry for Him and want you to tone it down until it is silenced. It is important to cry out all the more—keeping worldly influence off your life and bringing you out of darkness like blind Bartimaeus. His willingness to step out of his own security brought him a lasting change.

WHY SIT HERE

There was a severe famine in the land, and the prophet Elisha sent out word saying this time tomorrow the famine would be over. Things were about to change, and finally there would be enough to eat. Just outside the city gate sat four leprous men who began to reason with each other by saying, "Why sit we here until we die?" (2 Kings 7:3).

Strategizing a plan, they began to discuss their options: "If we go into the city, we will die because of the famine; if we stay sitting in this place, we also will die because there is nothing here for us either." So they decided to enter the camp of the Syrians because there was a small chance they would help them. They risked being killed—but they were going to die anyway, so they decided to take the chance. They figured it didn't matter; either way they were going to die.

Maybe this is your thinking. There aren't many options except to get up and move forward. These lepers had a choice to wait and die or to do something about it. Remember one of the first places that change is birthed in our lives is in our attitude. We have to make an effort. These four could have had an attitude, like many have, of "what's the use." But their attitude to press toward a change moved them toward victory, and it will move you too.

These lepers, like blind Bartimaeus, had to make a decision to no longer sit in the same place. They had to get up and be determined that tomorrow will be a new day—I will be different, I will be changed. In both examples of the four lepers and Bartimaeus, they had to be determined to move toward their change. When you move toward God and His Word because you don't want to stay the same, you will experience the change you so desperately desire.

Change is not always easy, and it requires effort. When I was a young boy, I had been picked on by someone in the neighborhood who was trying to make my life miserable. So one day I decided that I had had enough, and I scheduled a day with my opponent to have an official fight. I asked for the fight to be about a month in the future so I could have time to prepare. I started my training by lifting weights very diligently for the first few days, but then I quit. I couldn't stay consistent because I didn't see any immediate change or results. I gave up. I had committed to something that I wasn't putting an effort into, and my lack of effort was revealed on fight day.

I'll never forget that day. Kids came from all over to watch the duel, and it was over in only a few seconds, as my opponent immediately got the better of me. I had thought I was going to look like a bodybuilder in a few days without doing what it really takes to change.

Many battles are lost in our lives because we want change without consistently training or working for it. I have found that the key to change is found in a committed, consistent effort. The prodigal son in Luke 15 wanted his inheritance from his father and got it, but then he went and spent it on an unrighteous lifestyle. The initial excitement from his choice to live in sin eventually wore off, and something had to happen that finally brought him to the road of change and restoration. He had to come to a place where he wanted change no matter what it took to get it. Luke 15:17 says, "When he came to his senses…" (NIV). That meant that no matter how painful, or how much humbling or effort it required, he was at the end of himself and wanted a change. Often the only one standing in the way of our change to become more like Jesus is us. We have to get past ourselves, but it requires some effort and work.

Some refuse to change because they harden their hearts or think they can't change. Others enjoy the pleasure of their sinful lifestyle more than they desire to change. I once met privately with someone who, although I didn't realize at the time, had been committing adultery. Unknowingly I sat with them, sharing what I thought to be an unrelated story about another person in adultery and how God wanted that other person to change. I shared it as a spiritual example that related to our conversation, but God was using the story to speak to this person in front of me. The Lord was trying to extend His mercy for this person to change.

As I shared the story, tears fell from his eyes because he knew the Lord was reaching out and speaking to him prophetically through the story example. This was the opportunity to change. But this individual didn't take the forgiveness the Lord was offering. Sadly, he instead continued to sin. He didn't want to change no matter what it required of him.

On another occasion, I prophesied over a young person in a church service, telling her that the Lord was trying to reach out to her. I shared with this youth that she was dating someone whom she shouldn't be dating, and things were getting serious. This person was a Christian, but the person she had been dating was not pursuing God on the same level. As a sign, the Holy Spirit even supernaturally spoke the name of the person she was dating—God wanted this young person to change! Praise God, she did listen and change her mind. She didn't just sit around and do nothing. Like the four lepers and Bartimaeus, she did something about it. She moved toward change. And there are always rewards for changing in obedience to God.

Sow to Yourself Righteousness

Maybe you are saying to yourself, "I am ready to make changes in my life. Right now I want to go to a higher level in a sincere walk with the Lord that is not mixed with sin or compromise." Maybe it is a change like Bartimaeus's that moves you into victory over an area of discouragement and defeat. A key to your decision is found in Hosea 10:12, which says, "Sow to yourselves righteousness." This is speaking of a continual decision to plant seeds of righteousness into your life.

What exactly does that mean? First of all, Jesus taught that everything in the kingdom is based on the principle of sowing a seed. Sowing to yourself means that you make little decisions every day to do what is right. Each decision is like a little seed being sown. To sow righteousness into yourself, you make daily "seed decisions" of right living, right thinking, right attitudes, and right choices that will bring change so that you become more like Christ.

It is the seeds we plant daily in our lives that bring lasting, rewarding fruit. Many people want to live a life pleasing to the Lord, but they find themselves stumbling and defeated with the same things. It is the day-to-day choices and discipline that will help us please God in our walk with Him. Eli, a priest in the Bible, was severely dealt with by God because of his undisciplined sons who repeatedly committed sin out in the open for all to see. This grieved the Lord, and He was not pleased with Eli's choices to allow it to continue. He wouldn't do the day-to-day things necessary to bring the proper changes needed in his or his sons' lives.

When we make the daily choice to sow righteousness to ourselves, we will be challenged. Yes, we will often fail and find ourselves going to God to repent for the umpteenth number of times. I want to encourage you about something the Lord helped me with when it comes to repentance. I was having some attitudes with the Lord concerning another believer that I truly could not seem to get over. The Lord kept speaking to me about it because He didn't like it. I decided to try to change it, but on my terms and in my own way. The problem was that I was in control instead of God. I continued to fall short with it until I finally couldn't handle the conviction anymore.

Finally I said, "OK, Lord, I'm sorry for this." The Lord spoke back to me and said, "I am not looking for 'I'm sorry again,' Hank, but rather 'Lord, I repent.'" I asked the Lord the difference between the two. He told me that when I came to Him repeatedly apologizing, it wasn't repentance—I was sorry for my attitude, but I had no permanent intention to change it. True repentance is different. It is not just "I am sorry because I feel badly, but, when given the opportunity, I may do it again." That is an apology. Repentance is what God is after. He wants, "I don't like this sin; I repent and change my direction." It means you make a complete turnaround in your life.

Now, you might be saying, "I am trying to repent, but I can't seem to change after I repent." John the Baptist called many to repentance. In his call he gave us a little nugget of hope to stand on when it comes to repentance. In Matthew 3:8 he said, "Bring forth therefore fruits meet for repentance." In other words, he was saying have fruit in your life that shows you have truly repented. Well, the only way to have lasting fruit is to begin with seeds. Everything in the kingdom is about seeds. Once again, true repentance comes by the daily seed choices that eventually grow up to the lasting fruit of a changed life.

It is this daily decision of "I will not continue to sin by my choices today, Lord," that will bring about the results we want. This is what blind Bartimaeus did. He had a choice to make that would bring him out of the darkness of living blind into the light of being healed. It started with his choice to cry out to Jesus that day until he changed.

When I was in grade school, I once had a job that required pulling weeds that grew between some rocks on the side of a large hill. The hill was behind a business where my dad worked. It had so many weeds that it could potentially take all summer to pull them. Rather than spray the hill with weed killer, they hired my brother and me to do the pulling. I remember the first day we presented our boxes of weeds to show how many we had pulled. My dad's boss looked at our boxes and asked, "Where are the roots?" We were getting paid by the box and had pulled the tops off the weeds rather than getting to the roots. We had taken shortcuts in order to get paid sooner. It didn't take long to see that, because we didn't get to the roots, the weeds kept growing back until we were exhausted with our efforts in the hot summer sun.

From a spiritual perspective, many want to do the bare minimum to change and never get to the root of their problem. It keeps coming back because you never get to the source. You have to pull weeds before you can plant flowers. When we choose to make day-to-day choices in our hearts that get to the root, we position ourselves not for a "hill of weeds," but rather a life full of abundant fruit that brings glory to the Lord.

WHEN YOU ARE ALONE

One of the best ways to initiate change in our lives is by making right choices when no one else but God is watching. It is what we choose to do when we are alone. The true test of a man is not just what he does when he stands before many, but rather who he is when he is by himself. The devil loves to attack people when they are alone to sow things into their lives or convince them they will never change. The Bible tells us about many people who came under attack while they were alone. Satan waited for these opportunities to tempt them to fail.

- *David and Bathsheba:* "...at the time when kings go forth to battle..." (2 Samuel 11:1). David was supposed to go out to battle but instead stayed back. That decision set him up to lose another battle in his own life through the temptation to commit adultery with Bathsheba. While he was alone, he didn't protect his eye gates and gave into his fleshly desire to sin.

- *Eve, when tempted with forbidden fruit:* "And [the serpent] said unto the woman, Yea, hath God said, Ye shall not eat of every tree of the garden?" (Genesis 3:1). The devil attacked Eve while she was alone and got her to question God's Word. As a result, she didn't obey what God said. Instead, she reasoned with the devil, ate of the tree, and talked her husband into doing the same.

- *Joseph and Potiphar's wife:* "His master's wife cast her eyes upon Joseph; and she said, Lie with me. But he refused...How then can I do this great wickedness, and sin against God?" (Genesis 39:7–9). It is sad to say, but there are many people who would not have been as honorable as Joseph had they been in the same situation. Unlike David, however, he won the inward battle, which reveals something about his life. When no one was watching, he chose to make the right decision and avoid sin. He cared a great deal about the Lord's feelings on the matter. How many of us are like Joseph in that we are concerned or even aware of how the Lord feels about our choice to sin? Joseph is proof that we can overcome private temptations. He sowed to himself righteousness in the day-to-day decisions and therefore didn't give in to temptation. The inward conviction to do what was right was louder than the voice calling out to him through Potiphar's wife. That is amazing because the Bible said she wouldn't leave him alone about it. Genesis 39:10 says, "So it was, as she spoke to Joseph day by day, that he did not heed her, to lie with her or to be with her" (NKJV). Instead, he constantly looked for the door of escape. David didn't look for a door to escape his sexual temptation. He kept entertaining it and invited Bathsheba into his house. What we refuse to resist and then invite in our lives will eventually destroy us. But like Joseph, we can say, "I will not sin against God!" It all starts with your determination to change and overcome.

- *Samson and Delilah:* "And it came to pass afterward, that he loved a woman in the valley of Sorek, whose name was Delilah" (Judges 16:4). Samson flirted with sin by spending time alone with a harlot named Delilah. He should have never been alone with her. What we allow to consume the majority of our time while we are alone reveals what is our most important interest or affection. Samson didn't listen to the voice of conviction the way Joseph did. Instead, he placed his affection on the voice of Delilah calling out to him. Samson may have had outward strength, but he lacked the inward strength to say, "No!"

Of all of these four biblical examples, the only one who overcame their temptation was Joseph. Those who fell did so because they gave in to their flesh. The enemy hasn't changed in his methods of temptation. He still uses the lust of the eyes, the lust of the flesh, and the boastful pride of life. First John 2:16 says, "For all that is in the world, the lust of the flesh, and the lust of the eyes, and the pride of life, is not of the Father, but is of the world."

These are the things in the world that the devil uses to lure us away from God. Satan used them with Eve in the garden when he tempted her to eat from the tree. She looked at the tree and saw how pleasant it was. Then she desired its benefits. Ultimately the pride of life led her to eat it.

Notice the devil tried the same things with Jesus when he tempted Him. He used the lust of the eyes, the lust of the flesh, and the boastful pride of life, and Jesus resisted every effort. You have the same power over the enemy to resist temptation and defeat it. First Corinthians 10:13 tells us that there is always a way of escape when we are being tempted. We just have to look for that door. We have to look for a way to resist and get away from the temptation. According to the Bible, an escape route is always available. Sometimes we need to lay hands on our own head and say, "No! Just like Joseph, I will not sin against my Lord."

I asked the Father one day what He liked about Jesus. I know that He had many things, but His answer really blessed me. He said, "What I love about My Son is that He loved righteousness and hated sin." (See Psalm 45:7.) Do you know if the Lord loves that about Jesus, then He loves it about you too? This is yet another building block in not leaving God alone. We build a firm foundation in our hearts that hates sin the way God hates it.

When we were born again, the Bible says we became new creatures in Christ Jesus. Our spirit man was re-created in Christ, but we still live in a sinful, mortal, earthly body. Therefore, we have two natures. One is a sinful fleshly nature called the old man or our flesh. The other is a new nature, spiritually reborn, called the new man. Whichever one we feed and nurture the most will become the dominant one. If we feed the old man through an appetite for fleshly things, then he will become stronger and eventually dominate our actions. On the other hand, if we feed the new man spiritual things like the Word of God, worship, and prayer, then he will be the dominant one.

Every one of us has these two natures. That is why God changed the names of some people in the Bible. It painted a picture of change. They were changed people. We find Abram became Abraham, Sari changed to Sarah, Simon to Peter, and Saul became the apostle Paul, just to name a few. With a new nature came a new name to identify them.

We can overcome our old fleshly nature of sin when we choose to walk in the spirit and live a spiritual lifestyle. Don't leave God or yourself alone about it. It is time for a change. Try a few of the following things to help you overcome your fleshly nature and promote change.

- Come into God's presence through prayer and worship.
- Sow to yourself righteousness through daily choices.
- See your old nature dead. Think about it; a dead man doesn't sin.
- Put on the new ways of Christ just as you put on clothes.
- Starve your fleshly nature and feed your spirit.

EXPECT CHANGE

The reason some people never change is because when they ask God for a change, they don't truly expect it. Then others expect immediate results that generally don't manifest right away. Change is a process, and you have to make the choice to see it and step into it daily. Blind Bartimaeus being healed from blindness would require him to embrace a whole new lifestyle. He couldn't live like a blind beggar anymore. Everyone knew that he used to be blind, so now he would be expected to use his new vision for something productive. This meant a new occupation would be required and new clothing would be necessary. It could have meant he would have to learn a trade or skill. His experience with Jesus would require every area of his life to come into a new place of change and standard of living.

This is also true for those of us who once walked in spiritual darkness and blindness before we knew the Lord. In order to now walk in the true light of His kingdom, everything about us must now conform to His ways. We are expected to live like those who can see.

Now change isn't always easy. It reminds me of people who wear the same hairstyle or style of clothing for years, and everyone except them knows it is outdated. The problem is: they aren't open to any changes or suggestions. The truth is: they don't want to change. We become comfortable with who we are and how we have been living, whether it is right or wrong. People get set in their ways and become hardened to change.

When our church and ministry really began to grow, the Lord impressed on me to begin expecting changes. He let me know that what worked yesterday may not work today. You have to keep obtaining new levels in Him. This requires work and the willingness to change according to what the Lord wants. One day I picked up some loose coins I found, and these loose pieces of "change" once again made me think about fresh, new changes coming from the Lord. I literally started to notice everywhere I went that I would find change, loose coins, on the ground. I thought, "Wow, this is interesting that I keep finding loose change." Then I remembered that the Lord said to expect change. I soon realized He was using these coins to remind me of the change He was bringing to my life, our ministry, and the church congregation.

If we ask God to change us, we need to expect that He will get to work on it right away. One day I prophesied to a person and described what the Lord was showing me about the people he was hanging around. I told him, by the Holy Spirit, what he had been doing two days earlier and described the people he was with. I told him that the Lord said if he didn't change his choice to hang with these people, it would lead to him going to jail. God really ministered to him, and, thank God, he made the choice to change, even though it would require something from him. The others he had been hanging with did get in trouble, but not this person. He made a right choice to change and is pursuing ministry today! We must desire and expect to change regularly as we walk with God.

When God really changes you, your life will have the proof of that. Let's look again at blind Bartimaeus to see some things his miraculous change did for him.

True conversion

Mark 10:46 refers to him as "blind Bartimaeus." He had to be converted to a whole new identity. He went from living in darkness, or flesh, to a life of seeing. He could no longer be called blind. He was blind, and now he could see. This is conversion. Being truly converted is making Jesus your Lord and not just receiving Him as Savior. It is not just saying a prayer and continuing to live unchanged.

True disciple

Mark 10:46 says he "sat by the highway side begging." Verse 49 commands, "Rise; he calleth thee." And verse 50 states that Bartimaeus, "casting away his garment, rose, and came to Jesus." He went from sitting and begging to rising and following after Jesus. This is discipleship: denying yourself, no longer begging for handouts, but choosing to follow Christ.

True worshiper

Luke 18:43 says, "And immediately he received his sight, and followed him, glorifying God." Bartimaeus went from only thinking of himself to praising the Lord by "glorifying God." He became a worshiper instead of a beggar. A beggar's mentality is when everything is all about them. But a true worshiper's mentality is when it is all about Him.

True testimony

Luke 18:43 also tells us, "All the people, when they saw it, gave praise unto God." Bartimaeus became a testimony of the Lord's power and of a changed life. A changed life testifies of Jesus. It tells about His goodness and power to evangelize people.

All of these—conversion, discipleship, worship, and testimony—are evident when there is legitimate change.

CASTING OFF YOUR OLD GARMENTS

Once blind Bartimaeus made the scene he did by crying out to the Lord, it caused Jesus to stop in His tracks. Mark 10:49 says, "And Jesus stood still." There was something about Bartimaeus's cry of determination to not leave God alone that caused Jesus to stop and meet his need. If you will cry out from a true heart that desires to change at all costs, the Lord will take notice of you.

At first it appeared the Lord wasn't hearing him, but, in fact, Jesus was listening, and this man was about to be changed forever. It was more than a cry, however, that would cause a permanent change. There was an action required from Bartimaeus. It was a long-term heart decision that had to be revealed by his actions. Remember, Mark 10:50 said he cast off his garment and came toward Jesus. It represented a physical act of laying aside an old lifestyle.

A choice to change without action will not bring you the results you desire. Bartimaeus had to be determined not to allow the Lord to get away from him, so he would have to do something about it. Just like the stone of Lazarus that someone moved in order to bring a new life forward, Bartimaeus had to remove the garment of an old life. Many live under the garments of old mind-sets, habits, choices, and actions that must be laid aside and transformed in the Lord's image.

I was ministering in a service and the Holy Spirit had me speak to a man in the back row of the church. He really wasn't too sure about all of this "Spirit-filled stuff." So I told him that the Lord wanted to show Himself to be real to him and was about to give him a supernatural sign that would change his life. I said, "Sir, is this the name of the brand of cigarettes in your pocket?" And I named a brand of cigarettes to him. He immediately looked shocked and said, "Yes, sir." I told him that the Lord loved him and wanted to help him quit smoking if he wanted to. But more than that, God wanted to change his entire life. Now he could have reverted to fear at that point and held onto the old "garment" that was familiar to him. Instead, he got up and removed his old lifestyle to be gloriously changed by the Lord.

Change is something we have to be committed to every day of our Christian life. It is not something you decide once and for all. You keep making the choice to progress with the Lord. By doing so you will be a person who doesn't leave the Lord alone until you see change!

10

I Will Not Leave You Alone Until My Issues Stop

And a certain woman, which had an issue of blood twelve years, and had suffered many things of many physicians, and had spent all that she had, and was nothing bettered, but rather grew worse, when she had heard of Jesus, came in the press behind, and touched his garment.

—Mark 5:25–27

THE WOMAN IN this verse had her eyes fixed on the very One who could bring an end to twelve years of pain. No one had been able to help her, not even the doctors. Now, after spending all the money she had and receiving no improvement, she had become desperate. By now she was frail but determined not to leave God alone. She decided that if she could only reach far enough to touch the very bottom of His garment, that would be enough.

The only problem she faced now in order to make it happen was the large crowd standing between her and the Lord. How could she get to Jesus when she was so weak from years of bleeding? She didn't have the strength or the advantage of what others had as the rest of them thronged Jesus. As she was being pushed, knocked over, elbowed, and shoved, she kept her eyes on her goal. All she wanted was for her issue to stop.

Reaching with everything inside her, she pressed on toward the One who held the power for her healing. Couldn't anyone see her condition warranted special treatment and help her get ahead of the line? That would not be the case, however. To make matters more challenging, she was considered unclean according to the Law because of her condition. Now she was looked down on by the crowd of people who were pressing into the same thing she wanted. How could the issues of her life have any significance in the presence of so many? She kept reaching and inching closer, only to have her efforts constantly interrupted by the sheer size of the crowd.

Maybe this sounds familiar to you: "With so many people alive on the earth, how could my needs feel significant to the Lord? Surely He wants to attend to more important matters." Maybe you have been pressing forward, determined like this woman not to leave Him alone about your issue. You have pursued knowing that nothing else in your life matters more than having years of pain, struggle, and hopelessness end with just one experience with the Lord. You have been pushed aside, elbowed out, and shoved by life's circumstances and an enemy who doesn't want you to have your moment with Jesus. As a result, you have become nothing better but are growing worse.

There is hope for you! This woman's pursuit of her immediate miracle shows us an example that we can apply so we can see our issues stop.

The Bible tells us in Luke 8:40 that the people had been waiting for Jesus to arrive. They were excited and expecting the Lord to appear. This is how many people feel. They are waiting for the Lord to come and deal with their issues. Some have been like this woman, having issues for years. Maybe some of your issues are financial, health, marital, family, children, occupational, or church related that seem to never go away. You are desperate for the Lord to appear and do something.

This woman had spent all of her money on her condition, but she never improved. She needed a visit from Jesus. Yet, unlike the people in Luke 8:40, she didn't just wait for Him to appear. She decided to do something about it. She could have given in to all the hindrances in front of her. Look at the obstacles we need to avoid that will keep us bleeding and hemorrhaging with our issues:

- *Wrong words:* She could have easily talked about all the negative aspects of her situation. When you are uncomfortable or in pain, this is an easy trap to fall into. Her journey toward having her issue stop, however, began with her words. Matthew 9:21 says, "She said within herself, If I may but touch his garment, I shall be whole." According to Proverbs 4:20–23, God's Word produces the very forces of life. When we speak it from our mouth, it will affect our situation for good. We must never forget that we are the prophets of our own lives. What we speak over ourselves will come to pass.

- *Accepting the condition:* This woman suffered for twelve years, or one hundred forty-four months, with no help in sight. Passing time could have taught her to accept that it must have been God's will for her to be this way. The doctors said there was nothing they could do. But she didn't accept her condition. She determined to take action and do something. She wasn't going to leave Jesus alone and let Him pass by her without getting a miracle.

- *Discouragement by people and surrounding circumstances:* The woman could have easily said, "This crowd is too big, and I might get hurt." The truth is, the crowd was huge, and she was risking an injury by getting in the middle of it. Still she didn't let that stop her, and she didn't use the surrounding circumstances as an excuse. People and circumstances around you can discourage you from trying.

They can hinder the answer to your issues by acting as a barrier between you and your breakthrough.

- *Self-isolation:* The Bible never says she had anyone come along to help her. She was on her own to chase down her miracle. She was unclean to everyone who saw her, and they probably judged her for it. She could have isolated herself because of fear and intimidation, but instead she came to Jesus for a solution to her issue.

- *Self-pity:* She could have easily had a pity party and used the excuse that no one understood how she was feeling. Was her pain real? Yes. Was her condition serious? Yes. But she wasn't going to keep feeling sorry for herself and possibly miss out on her healing. She had to look past her present feelings and see a future miracle. She didn't cry and stay home waiting for Jesus to come for her and then use that as an excuse for why she didn't receive anything. No, she went against the odds and pursued her blessing until she got what she wanted.

- *Hopelessness:* Having tried to find a cure for the last twelve years, she could have also fallen into a state of hopelessness. Sometimes when we feel that we have already tried everything there is, we are unwilling to look into one more thing. We cease to care after many failed attempts and an empty bank account. She decided to see the things people were saying about Jesus as more than just a rumor or another futile try for a cure. She didn't give in to hopelessness, but she decided to keep herself in pursuit of her breakthrough.

I once went to preach on the streets outside the city auditorium just as a rock concert was getting out. I was with a street witnessing team, and we decided to wait until the concert was over so people would see our ministry not as a protest but as an outreach instead. The night before the concert, I heard the Holy Spirit tell me to go pray around the auditorium to prepare the grounds for ministry. I did as He instructed.

Just after the concert, we started reaching out to people with the gospel. I decided to jump up onto a medium-sized retaining wall and then call out to people passing by and preach to them. The anointing of the Holy Spirit was strong, and people began listening to me. At first I was a little uncomfortable because of the size of the crowd—and this certainly wasn't a Christian preaching meeting.

Toward the end of my preaching, I noticed a small stir in the back of the crowd as a man came staggering toward me with some difficulty because of the large number of people. He finally made it after quite an effort of pushing and shoving his way through until he was standing directly in front of me, soaked in blood from his head down to his face and chest. Someone had broken glass over his head, and he was visibly drunk. As he was looking up at me, I reached my hand out to pray for him. It reminded me of the woman with the issue of blood pushing her way forward to receive her miracle. I leaned over the wall and touched this man, rebuking the devil from his life, and then commanded the bleeding to stop. He started to fall under the power as some of the team members caught him. Immediately his issue of blood stopped, and he became sober. What a sight! This was incredible, and I was able to lead many others to Christ because they saw a miracle with their own eyes.

God does not see your situation any differently from that of the man I ministered to in the crowd that day, or even from that of the woman with the issue of blood. What the Lord did for them, He will do for you if you continue to reach out. No matter what you are facing, press through and don't leave God alone until your miracle comes.

Nothing Better but Growing Worse

The more this woman with the issue of blood tried to get help, the worse her condition seemed to become. Her only answer now was to touch Jesus. Mark 5:26 says she "had suffered many things of many physicians, and had spent all that she had, and was nothing bettered, but rather grew worse." What a hopeless feeling it is when there is no one left to help you and the situation is continually progressing from bad to worse.

This woman had reached that point in her life. Doctors are practitioners who really don't possess real power to heal anyone outside of God. They simply practice medicine. What this woman needed was not a touch from powerless men but a touch from the true physician, Jesus Christ. This woman had nowhere to turn but to God. He alone had the answer. The only way to stop the downward spiral of things getting worse was in her choice not to leave God alone. Her eyes were on Him to touch Him.

When you feel you are in a situation that seems to only be getting worse, that is the time—more than ever—to keep your eyes fixed on Jesus. Out of desperation, some people begin to search for other things to make them happy or to be their answer to life's issues. It feels like the Lord is too far off in the distance, and it will be difficult to get His attention. What action will you take as your circumstances deteriorate? With everything happening in the world today, people need to realize that things will only get worse if they try to keep solving their problems without God and a serious commitment to Him.

One time I had gone to the doctor for a very serious cough that seemed to be getting worse after each visit. It was a persistent cough that the doctors said was some kind of virus, but they didn't seem to know what it was or if they could cure it. They just kept giving me medicines to treat it. I would literally cough violently and uncontrollably with any change in temperature—getting in and out of the shower, going outside in the winter weather. Laughter would trigger these episodes too. It finally got so bad, and I would cough so hard that I would suddenly throw up. It was awful.

I look back with some humor now at one episode when I took my wife to dinner at a nice restaurant. It was very cold that night, so as soon as we walked outside from the restaurant, one of these episodes hit me. It came on so quickly, I had no choice but to bend over and cough up my entire dinner in the bushes just outside the restaurant's front door. This occurred just as another couple was walking inside to eat. I'm sure they wondered what kind of food they served there.

The doctors told me I had to keep trying different pills because they didn't know quite what the ailment was. I remember the hopeless feeling as I drove home one night from the doctor's office. I finally told my wife, Brenda, that I'd had enough. I didn't want to spend the rest of my life taking medicine. It wasn't until we got righteously angry at the devil that we became tenaciously determined about our healing covenant with God. I was getting worse, and I needed to go to God and press into Him until I got a breakthrough. Brenda and I got our Bibles out and prophesied and spoke God's Word to my condition. Then every time I would start to cough, we commanded the issue to stop in Jesus's name. After a short period of not leaving God alone about it, victory came. But I had to see that, in a situation that was only getting worse, I needed to pursue after the Lord's promises and be firmly settled in them.

The Bible tells us, in 1 Samuel 30, about a time in King David's life that he had an issue he was faced with that couldn't have gotten any worse. He had just come home with many of his mighty men after a battle fought in Ziklag. When they arrived, they discovered that their homes were on fire and their wives and children had been kidnapped by an enemy.

What would they do? They were so upset at the horrific sight that they began to cry. Were their families even still alive? It was so bad, David's mighty men even considered stoning him because of what happened to their homes and families. They had been so loyal to fight battles, many with him, but they were now blaming him. David did something, however, that turned a bad day into a good day and stopped his terrible issue. This is key for you and me as we, like the woman with her issue, press toward our victory.

The key was David didn't continue weeping; he ran to God in the middle of this terrible issue. He made the journey to touch the Lord. He faced his issues with the help of the Lord, and that is how he was able to encourage himself. (See 1 Samuel 30:6.) His strength to handle this great problem was found in the Lord. As a result, he found the answer he was looking for to deal with his issue. The answer God gave David to handle his issues was not one of retreat, but one of pursuing, overtaking, and recovering all that was stolen. David did exactly as the Lord instructed, and his issues stopped. All his stolen property was returned because his trust was in the Lord during a bad situation.

What is amazing is the prophetic significance of David's mighty men. The fact that they wanted to stone him during an issue but were equally a part of the solution to stop the issue is worth further examination. They carried some powerful qualities necessary if we are going to be able to stop issues too. Adino, Eleazar, Shammah, and Benaiah were men to whom God granted victory by their special areas of expertise listed in 2 Samuel 23:

Adino: "He lift up his spear against eight hundred, whom he slew at one time" (verse 8). He didn't give up at any point, not after killing fifty, one hundred, two hundred, or even five hundred. He didn't quit. He was outnumbered 800 to 1. He didn't give up even when the odds were against him. His refusal to surrender to the enemy and the feeling of being outnumbered led to his victory. We can learn from this warrior, Adino, just as we can learn from the woman with the issue of blood who was outnumbered in her chance to touch Jesus with so many in front of her. Neither of them gave up when the odds were against them, and you don't have to either.

Eleazar: "The son of Dodo…attacked the Philistines until his hand was weary, and his hand stuck to the sword" (verses 9–10, NKJV). We also have to hold on to our sword, which is the Word of God (Ephesians 6:1). You will see victory when you apply God's Word to your situation. The Bible is one of the greatest spiritual weapons God has given to us to deal with life's issues. We can learn from Eleazar that he knew how to hold on to his sword when faced with an attack. The woman with the issue of blood held on to her answer—the garment of Jesus—until her issues stopped.

Shammah: He stood and defended his ground even after others fled from their post (2 Samuel 23:11–12). He was willing to face his battle alone, without help. He didn't let it keep him from fighting forward. We can learn from Shammah and the woman with the issue, who were both alone to face their battles. Even when you have to go it alone, victory will come if we stand our ground and refuse to give up. They both stood during a crisis and were determined to get a victory. Even when you feel alone at your post, if you don't leave God alone, He is there to help you. Though others may have fled, God is still there for you.

Benaiah: He slew a lion with his own sword and then stole his enemy's spear and used it to defeat him, all during the time of snow (verses 20–22). He didn't wait for the ideal conditions. It was cold and snowy. Sometimes the time of snow in our lives is when things seem cold, lifeless, and hopeless. The conditions are opposing you. Benaiah and the woman with the issue of blood were able to find victory in less than perfect conditions. Then what the enemy tried to use against them, they defeated. They took the enemy's weapon and used it against him. The conditions may not seem ideal for a miracle, but that victory will come if we refuse to leave God alone.

We can apply the same principles as these mighty men and become strong in the Lord to overcome the issues we face in our lives. You can be like Adino and fight even when the odds are against you, or Eleazar, and not let go of your sword and what you believe. Then also become like Shammah; when everyone else quits and gives up, you refuse. Then learn to fight your battles no matter what the conditions surrounding you are like, just the way Benaiah did.

REACH OUT AND DON'T LET HIM GO

Even if you are pursuing God about your issue, there will come a point when you will have to reach out with your hand and touch Him. You will have to connect yourself to His power. This means that you will often have to make an open decision to take ahold of the anointing. You will have to reach out for help and may not be able to keep your internal problem hidden any longer. This woman was hemorrhaging from the inside out. This is important if we want our issues—whether obvious or hidden—to cease.

This woman's inward issues eventually came out and were visible to all as she had to make her way into the crowd. She tried to quietly touch Jesus, but her reaching out to Him was going to be an unhidden matter (Luke 8:47). We cannot always stay in our private corner of secrecy if we are truly going to be touched by the power of God. God is not into embarrassing anyone, but sometimes the only way to get to the root problem is to dig into the ground and bring some things to the surface. We can't hide our issues. They will eventually come out if we refuse to deal with them. This woman apparently tried to get healed without anyone noticing. Whether in a private meeting with a pastor, another believer, or even in a church service setting, decide that no matter what people might think, you are going to make contact with the power of God.

Not only did people know about her issue when she touched Jesus, but also she had to initiate the action of touching His garment. Her issues were no longer hidden; neither was her shame. Her decision to be open about her problem in front of the crowd that day resulted in her healing. Oftentimes many hope that their issues will go away, or they don't want to deal with them, so they run away from their answer rather than run to it. They don't want anyone to think badly of them, so they don't come up for the prayer line or altar call. They don't want to deal with an issue because someone might see them reach out to the power of God about it.

The problem is that an issue will eventually become a life-threatening hemorrhage. Unless you get it stopped, it will slowly drain the entire life out of your walk with God. Leviticus 17 says the life of all flesh is in the blood. This woman was hemorrhaging and losing life. This is exactly how some feel when they are having issues. The life and excitement in their Christianity is being drained, and the only thing they know is pain. If we choose to cover up our present state, we will never be able to face our future. When this woman reached out to the power of God, when it came by her, she touched her future.

Notice that when her issue was seen by all, Jesus didn't embarrass her or turn her away. She had been considered unclean—the equivalent to a modern-day sinner—but her reaching out made her a candidate for a miracle. Remember God's promise in Psalm 103:10: "He hath not dealt with us after our sins; nor rewarded us according to our iniquities." This woman felt afraid, ashamed of her condition. You must not let embarrassment make you feel crowded out by others and less important to God. You are special and important to Him. How far are you willing to reach? What distance are you willing to follow in order to see Him turn to you and meet your need?

My wife and I often minister together in the spirit. One may preach while the other moves in the power of God, or vice versa. Other times one may speak out a tongue over someone, or something, while the other one interprets it. In one service, I was ministering over people in tongues around the audience and my wife was interpreting the tongues. In this case, I knew the situations of some of the people I had called out, even though I try not to call people out for this type of ministry based on what I know about them. I was expecting the Lord to speak something to really address some of their issues and perhaps even express some of His possible disagreement with certain lifestyles. I was expecting a more confrontational interpretation of the tongue than was coming by the Holy Spirit.

Instead, what the Lord said and how He ministered was so beautiful. The interpretation through my wife was so specific but remained very encouraging. God does not always address things the way we expect. He was definitely trying to bring His mercy and truly help those being ministered to that day. The Lord is not out to embarrass you or make you feel condemned when you are there to reach out to Him. If you are truly trying to get your heart right and seek Him, He will extend His love to you. He won't be there to condemn or embarrass you.

"WHO TOUCHED ME?"

In the story of the woman with the issue of blood, so many people passed by pushing to touch Him, but only one got recognized for it. That means it is possible that some ways we touch Him have greater impact than others. What are some things we can do to cause Him to stop and recognize our touch? I am sure in your heart you want God to notice your efforts to touch Him. This woman heard Him say, "Who touched me?" This is one of the greatest things we can hear Him say to us. He doesn't want to be alone. He wants us to touch Him until His power is released on our need. He is looking for those who, like this woman, will stand out from the rest.

"Jesus said, 'Who touched me?'" (Luke 8:45, NKJV). What a statement! While hundreds were thronging the Lord, her touch was felt in a special way. You are special and your needs are important to God, but how do you get Him to notice you in the midst of a busy, crowded earth? Look at what this woman did to get His attention.

- *Initiated contact:* "She said within herself, If I may but touch..." (Matthew 9:21). She got His attention because she wasn't just looking for Him to touch her, but she initiated the contact in reaching for Him. Those who really don't leave God alone will initiate contact with God rather than wait around for a touch from Him.

- *Pressed toward Him:* After twelve long years, she pressed through the crowd. This number twelve represents kingdom. It means she pressed into the kingdom. Because she pressed into it, she found her healing and Jesus noticed that effort. Luke 16:16 says the kingdom of God is preached and every man presses into it. We can press by seeking Him or reading the Bible when we don't feel like it. We press by our heart attitude and actions; even when our issues seem overwhelming, we keep going toward the Lord.

- *No other options:* She completely abandoned herself to Him because there was no other choice but Him! She had already tried everything else out there. Those who don't leave God alone will make Him a priority in their life rather than an afterthought. They decide He is the only solution.

- *Believed her words:* Notice that she was confident in her words. She said, "...I shall be whole" (Matthew 9:21). She believed it enough that she put actions behind what she believed. The Bible said she came behind Him as He was going a different direction—He was positioned to overlook her because she was behind Him. Didn't He see her? Was He ignoring her? None of that mattered to her, and she didn't make it a case as so many Christians do with the

Lord. But it provoked all the more response of faith in her, and it made Jesus take notice.

Now why do you suppose she determined to touch the hem of His garment? Perhaps from a literal perspective, it was the easiest thing for her to grasp. From a prophetic view, however, the hem of a garment is the strongest part since it has a double layer of fabric. She needed to exchange her strength for His strength. Isn't that what the Bible teaches, that those who wait on the Lord will be renewed with strength? She also touched the hem of His garment because, in order to touch this bottom part, you have to be at your lowest point.

This woman was truly at her lowest point of need. Luke 8:44 says she "touched the edge of his cloak" (NIV). The word *edge* in the Greek is the word *kraspedon*, which means "the border or hem of the garment." In Numbers 15:38 it was referred to as the tassels or fringes that the Jewish rabbis wore on the four corners of the cloak. These corners of the cloak or tassels were also called "wings." This is a common reference in Jewish tradition when speaking about the prayer shawl worn by the priests. It gives a new meaning to the scripture in Malachi 4:2, which says He will "arise with healing in his wings." Additionally, we see a fresh revelation in Psalm 91:4 when it says, "Under his wings shalt thou trust." This woman was not only going to find healing from Christ's priestly ministry, at her lowest point of need, but she was also going to find strength and refuge. Your place of refuge is to reach out and touch His presence and garment of strength.

I want to say just a few more things about the way the woman with the issue of blood initiated her contact with the hem of Jesus's garment. She made the contact, not Him, which is a picture of the mature person or Christian. In most of the church, we have it turned around. We wait for a "touch" from God. Now it's not that He will not touch us, but our initiating contact with His power will cause

Him to turn and acknowledge our need. When this woman touched Jesus, she received special attention from Him. Those who don't leave God alone get special attention. He is a rewarder of those who diligently seek Him (Hebrews 11:6).

It takes maturity and commitment to not leave God alone and not be afraid to initiate the pursuit or contact. Now, in Luke 8:41–42 there were two females in need of a touch, both, interestingly enough, with the number twelve mentioned. There was the woman with the issue of blood for twelve years, and a little twelve-year-old girl who was dying. There is even another prophetic significance to the number twelve being mentioned in both of their situations. The Bible could have left that detail out of their stories, but for good reason did not. Twelve is the number that represents the kingdom of God because His kingdom (the church) began with twelve elders—the twelve apostles of the Lamb. So there is a kingdom message to the church in the stories about these two females.

The first was the woman with the issue of blood that she had for twelve years. This prophetically represents the Lord's church and believers—who are supposed to be mature. They have been part of the body of Christ for years but have issues that hinder their spiritual lives, even though they have had plenty of time to do something about those issues. Many can never seem to be free from the same old things; others can't seem to reach a higher place in God or are waiting to be touched by God rather than press into Him.

Remember, the sign of a true, mature believer is not one who always needs to feel, see, or experience something. It's not even having the pastor available to touch you for every need or problem. A mature believer initiates the time with God and learns that they don't have to wait to be touched. They initiate pursuit of the power of God no matter what they are facing.

Secondly, we see a young girl who was twelve. The fact that she was

189

a child speaks of the church and believers who never come to a place of maturity. They die before they grow into their full destiny with God. They live most of their Christianity depending on everyone else to meet their needs; thus they are not maturing as Christians. These people don't touch God or initiate time with Him. They only want their needs to be met first. Early on in their spiritual lives, they "die" in their Christian experience, and many are no longer in the church.

This young girl was not yet mature and needed to receive her healing by Jesus touching her. (See Luke 8:54.) Baby Christians need the help of the ministry to mature them or they will die. Of course, all of us need the help of a local church to keep us on track with the Lord, but babies need special care.

So the grown woman with an issue was healed when she initiated contact with God. The young girl was healed when she received a touch from the mature ministry of Jesus. Both are needed in the kingdom of God so we can be set free by His power.

Virtue Is Still Available Today

The virtue and power that the woman with the issue of blood received are still available today. If you read Luke 8 and 9, you see that the hidden lesson in the story of the two girls continues. The number twelve appears again, but now it is in reference to the twelve disciples—speaking further of the church. Jesus was giving them power to do something. Now the touch from Jesus is represented in the twelve (the church) being sent with power. They were no longer just initiating contact, nor were they just waiting for a touch, but they were about to take the power and go someplace with it.

There comes a point when we have to take the power—the virtue Jesus gave us—and touch someone else. A mature church is not one who is dying or hemorrhaging with issues, but one who will now touch the world.

This power or virtue is available to you and in you to touch others. This is God's ultimate goal: for us to mature and touch someone else. Now we can become the "garment," the body of Christ, for someone else to touch. We have been given power—just like Jesus—that when people come to us with a problem, no matter what it is, the power of God within us will make that problem stop. Then, also through God's power, we can pass that same power and virtue on to them so they may do the same for others.

I love watching believers lay hands on the sick and seeing people recover. I get excited for them to prophesy, operate in the gifts of the Spirit, cast out devils, minister the Word of God, and do the works of the ministry. This is what we have been created for, to display His power to this generation. We are born for signs and wonders. (See Isaiah 8:18.) People that want God's power are hungry. They realize that powerless religion can't help them. They are looking for you and me to show them the power of God.

I tell you, I have seen so many times in meetings when people are desperately reaching out for the power of God. Many times I have ministered and watched marvelous healings and miracles take place in meetings. Then even after the meeting, people are still trying to reach out and touch the power of God on you. This is what God wants us to be, a source of virtue for their healing. We need to progress from Luke 8, like the two women, and move into Luke 9:1. There is a world desperately waiting for our virtue to touch them.

Realize that God wants your issues to stop today. And if you have been dealing with the same thing for many years, there is hope for you. You are special to Him, and your issues can stop. Then you can carry the virtue to help others with *their* issues. Initiate contact with the power of God today. Say within yourself that no matter how you feel or what you face, you are not going to leave God alone until the issues plaguing your life are no more. Say, "I will be made whole, and my future will be forever changed. I am important to God, and He is about to take notice of me." Then expect your life to change into His image. Don't be afraid to touch other's lives and teach them how to not leave God alone until their issues stop!

11

How to Not Leave God Alone

> God created man in his own image, in the image of God
> created he him; male and female created he them....And
> the Lord God said, It is not good that the man should be
> alone; I will make him an help meet for him.
>
> —Genesis 1:27; 2:18

THE BIBLE SAYS, in the very beginning of time God created the entire heavens and the earth in just a few short days. His most intimate creation, however, would be the most special and look just like Him. Genesis 1:27 says He fashioned something that was actually going to think, walk, and talk just like Him. This masterpiece would be known as mankind. This special creation was given everything the Lord had made for His own enjoyment. There was still one thing missing, though. There was no one else in human form created in Adam's image.

It wasn't right for man to be alone without anyone else on Earth who could relate to him on his level. God knew that man had that need inside of him because man was an exact copy of His own image. There was a day when God was alone, without anyone else like Himself to commune with. God did not want to be alone, so He made man. He knew man would have these same feelings, so the Lord created Eve, Adam's helper, the one to help meet his longing for a companion: "I will make him an help meet for him" (Genesis 2:18).

God knew Adam didn't want to be alone because He knew for Himself what it was like to be alone. Just as He made Eve for Adam's companionship, He made people for His companionship. I believe before God said, "It is not good that the man should be alone," He said inside Himself, "I don't want to be without companionship. It is not good for Me to be alone." God wanted a friend like Himself—for Himself—to satisfy the longing in His heart.

That longing created mankind. We are made for His fellowship. Now He would never have to be alone. In the same way God pulled Adam out from an inward place of Himself, God also brought forth Eve from inside of Adam. Now Adam would not be alone.

Do you realize we were created for the express purpose of fellowship with God? He loves us and wants to be with us. So now the question remains, how do we go about never leaving God alone?

Teach Us to Not Leave You Alone

Of course, with a little different twist on it, this question was brought to Jesus in Luke 11:1, when one of His disciples asked Him about prayer, saying, "Lord, teach us to pray." The disciple recognized that knowing how to pray was a secret to power. He wanted to know the secrets of connecting with God—not leaving Him alone. Prayer, after all, is not just speaking words into empty space. It is connecting with a very real and powerful God who is waiting for us to respond to His love. That is the crux of what prayer is all about. It is wanting to be with God.

This disciple most certainly saw this in Jesus's life. He saw the many hours Jesus talked with the Father. It was more than just prayer; it was relationship with God so committed that God was never left alone.

When Adam and Eve sinned in the garden, they left God alone by hiding from Him. Of course, God knew where to find them and, even though separated through sin, was already planning the way to call them back to Him. He devised a plan so He would not be alone again. He sent Jesus to let us know we could be reconnected with Him. Jesus is the answer to our relationship to almighty God. He knows how to connect us with Him. That is why He taught on prayer—He taught us the keys to connect with God, so the Lord will never be alone. He taught us the four main categories—the keys—to make sure God is never left alone.

Category 1: Your personal relationship with the Father

Luke 11:2 says, "When ye pray, say, Our Father..." Your ability to not leave God alone begins with your Father! He is not just someone else's Father, but *your* Father. That means you talk with Him, spend time with Him, and meet with Him. You have to plan for it and make a place for it. It is difficult to truly know your Father if you never set a time and determine a meeting place. Second Chronicles 7:14 tells us to seek His face. Seeking His face means we study His features and His character, and we know what He is like. We learn His expressions and understand how His power will work to help us. Jesus set this example in His own life on Earth. He sought God's face so much that He was able to be a picture of God for us. Jesus said, "If you have seen me, you have seen the Father" (John 14:9, CEV.) He knew what the Father was like because He spent time with Him.

Category 2: Praying for others

Luke 11:5–6 says, "Which of you shall have a friend, and shall go unto him at midnight, and say unto him, Friend, lend me three loaves; for a friend of mine in his journey is come to me, and I have nothing to set before him?" Jesus teaches another principle about not leaving God alone that is found in praying for others. He illustrates this by sharing a story of a friend who was going to make certain his guest was taken care of. His persistence even in the middle of the night brought blessing both for himself and someone else.

Category 3: Persistence in prayer

In Luke 11 Jesus shows us a third category called importunity or persistence: "Because of his importunity..." (verse 8). "Ask...seek, and...knock..." (verse 9). It is found in continual asking that does not quit until you receive something. Seek and keep seeking, even when it seems you aren't getting an answer. Knock and keep on knocking, even though it seems the doors to heaven aren't opening. It's your importunity—your willingness to not give up and to not leave Him alone—that causes the blessing to be released.

Category 4: Overcoming the enemy

In Luke 11:20–28, this entire passage talks about binding the strongman or enemy. God will not be left alone when you bind the forces of darkness trying to separate you from Him. It is found in your willingness to resist the enemy and fight for your time with God. When you take authority over the devil and don't give in to His temptations, you will stay close and connected with God.

DON'T BOTHER ME

After Jesus divided our prayer focus into four categories, He again taught another practical principle about not leaving God alone:

> Then he said, "Imagine what would happen if you went to a friend in the middle of the night and said, 'Friend, lend me three loaves of bread. An old friend traveling through just showed up, and I don't have a thing on hand.' The friend answers from his bed, 'Don't bother me. The door's locked; my children are all down for the night; I can't get up to give you anything.' But let me tell you, even if he won't get up because he's a friend, if you stand your ground, knocking and waking all the neighbors, he'll finally get up and get you whatever you need."
>
> —Luke 11:5–8, THE MESSAGE

The friend in this story is God. Jesus tells this story about a man who has a visiting friend coming at midnight, and he has nothing to feed him. This man, who has nothing to give his houseguest to eat, goes at the midnight hour to knock on a neighboring friend's door and asks to borrow some food for his visitor. He asks for three loaves of bread. This prophetically represents the Father, the Son, and the Holy Ghost. They are the source we need to provide others to feed on. This bread of God is given to every man who hungers for it. It is available twenty-four hours a day, seven days a week, as often as we need it. And asking for bread at midnight tells us that God is there for us anytime, regardless of the hour.

The problem with the friend in this story is that he yelled back through the door, "Don't trouble me or bother me. The door is shut, my children are asleep, and it is late; I don't want to wake them." This neighbor doesn't seem like he wants to be bothered. I am sure the guy knocking on the door could have felt irritated that he was being ignored or pushed away. Could that picture really represent God? How can God ignore my request? What kind of friend is He anyway? Can't He see I have an immediate need and so does my guest? Yes, it can feel at times like God is ignoring your knock at the door.

As we have seen in other examples in this book, God acts like this friend on purpose at times. He may appear too far for our reach, or that He doesn't want to be bothered. No, He wants to provoke a persistent response! Let me refresh your memory about some of the other examples we have covered so far. Remember when God wrestled with Jacob, even trying to make him let go? Then there was Moses, whom God told to leave Him alone. How about the four-hundred-year cry from the children of Israel before a God who seemed to take forever to answer their need for a deliverer? Oh, then there was Lazarus, whom Jesus loved as a friend but didn't run to at his dying moment.

What about the blind beggar Bartimaeus, who wanted to change from a life of darkness to light? It seemed his cry wasn't being heard as Jesus was leaving and walking away from his need. We can't forget the woman with the issue of blood who wanted her problems to end. Jesus didn't even stop to touch her—He walked away in a different direction. This woman had to initiate the contact to get Him to even notice. I believe these examples echo the friend who wouldn't rise at midnight to give the knocking friend any bread. And all of these appear that the Lord didn't go out of His way or even want to be bothered.

Is this what He really wants? Does God want to be left alone? Of course not! He is waiting for our response to provoke us to pursue Him of our own free will and choice.

Would this friend at midnight respond to the voice from outside his door and meet his need? Couldn't the one knocking understand he didn't want to be bothered? He said, "Don't trouble me." This friend—God—is trying to get this knocking neighbor to learn something about what it means to not quit, to not leave Him alone or give up his effort. Well, in the story he learned the lesson. He persisted to get the desired result.

This is exactly what God wants us to do. Jesus continues teaching in Luke 11:9 how to not leave Him alone and get the answers we need. First, He tells us to ask and come to Him. Secondly, He says to seek Him daily and build a friendship so that we can confidently come to Him at all hours and for what we need in any situation—just as we saw in the story of the knocking neighbor who needed bread. Then, lastly, He teaches us to go ahead and knock because the answer is ours and lies just behind the door. God doesn't want to be alone, and He looks for the persistent ones who will knock on the door and press into His kingdom.

Jesus used this example in Luke 11:2–4 to teach the disciples, and us, how to press in when we pray. And He gave us the words to speak, teaching us the principles of relationship with God and answered prayer.

- Our Father (verse 2). The first thing He taught was to pray and get to know God by calling Him "Our Father—*your* Father." It personalizes your relationship.

- Hallowed be Thy name (verse 2). We increase the intimacy of relationship through worship. It is how we express our love when we reach out to Him.

- Thy kingdom come, Thy will be done on Earth as it is in heaven (verse 2). Individuals who don't leave God alone will make His purposes their priority. They are concerned that His will is established in their lives over their own plans and desires in life.

- Give us our daily bread (verse 3). This is an expression of total dependence on Him for all your needs. It means we "feed" first on Him for our supply. Our hunger is satisfied in the Lord. The children's bread is healing, blessing, and deliverance.

- Forgive us of our sins as we forgive others (verse 4). We can't allow sin to keep us separated from Him. Even when we fail, we need to run to Him. Adam and Eve hid from God when they sinned. Don't be ashamed; you can ask the Lord to forgive you and have confidence about it because you already cultivate forgiveness in your heart for other people. This spirit of forgiveness will also help us to escape temptation and be confident to pray "deliver us from evil."

I Will Not Take No for an Answer

When Jesus taught about importunity in Luke 11, He was imparting to us the attitude of not taking no for an answer. The word *importunity* actually means, "to be shameless, bold, determined, pressing, entreating, and being persistent in requesting." Jesus taught much about persistence or "importunity." This is why He told us to pray and not faint in Luke 18:1. He wanted us to become people who never give up.

We must continue to persist, press in prayer, and be confident we will receive an answer if we determine not to grow weary. That is why He used the story about the friend who appeared to not want to be troubled. The Lord wants to see if you will not take no for an answer. He wants to see how much you will persist to receive your anticipated blessing.

The friend who knocked at midnight reveals the heart of those who refuse to leave God alone and who will keep seeking Him until He answers. The friend was unwilling to take no for an answer and kept knocking and being persistent until his neighbor came, opened the door, and gave him what he needed. He was willing to risk it all by launching out at a late hour and expecting his need to be met.

I learned an amusing example about being persistent and not taking no for an answer. It was a natural lesson in my life that taught me the importance of spiritual persistence. One time I was planning a trip to watch a college football bowl game that was almost impossible to get tickets for. Unable to get a ticket beforehand, I was not going to give up on seeing this game. A willing friend and I left on an airplane, without tickets and without a hotel room, to a sold-out football game. What are the chances of getting in to watch a game like that, or even having a place to sleep that night? We wanted to go so badly that we decided to take the risk. I guess I figured I had better pray about it, but I had trust that the Lord was going to bless us when we got there.

I make a regular habit of believing for His blessing and favor, so I just naturally felt confident that God was going to do a miracle.

When we arrived, we flagged down a taxi. I will never forget that crazy cab driver. He asked us where we wanted to go. I told him we didn't know; we came to watch the game, hoping to get tickets, so we asked him to drive us to the hotel nearest to the stadium.

"What? My common sense tells me you have made big mistake," he said in broken English. He told us all the hotels were full and we would not find a place to stay, nor would we be able to get tickets to the game because everything in town was sold out.

This one-way conversation went on for a long time until I finally said, "Look, sir, drive us to the hotel closest to the stadium. We will get a room, plus we are getting tickets on the fifty-yard line."

He laughed and said, "Crazy! You are crazy, my common sense tells me..."

I interrupted and told him, "My heart said we will get a room and tickets on the fifty-yard line. I talked to Jesus about it, and I believe that I am in for His blessing. Now please just do what I ask."

"OK! OK!" he said. "But my common sense tells me..."

We finally arrived at the hotel lobby and went to the front desk, only to be informed that there were no rooms and all the hotels around town were full. Then I heard that crazy driver again say, "See I told you my common sense says..."

I started to turn around and leave until a man came out from behind the counter and said, "Sir, sir!" As he tried to flag me down, he said, "You won't believe this, but I just got a call from someone staying here and they have to leave. You can have their room and, by the way, they have two tickets on the fifty-yard line for sale at face value!"

My friend and I began to praise the Lord. All this persistence and trusting God paid off. The Lord answered our prayers. You know what I did? That's right. I respectfully went back to my commonsense taxi driver, who was shaking his head, saying, "I can't believe it." I told him about Jesus and encouraged him to give his life to the Lord. Determining to hold on to God's promise oftentimes won't make any sense to others, and may not make any common sense at all. It is in persistence that we find our blessings.

Looking back on that humorous adventure, I did learn a powerful truth. We endured some great challenges in our trust that the Lord would answer our prayers. We had to continue to persevere not taking no for an answer. It makes me consider what would happen if we approached God that way on a regular basis.

The questions needing to be asked are: How persistent are you? Will you be like the man who knocked at midnight? Will you leave God alone and walk away even if it appears your prayers aren't being answered or you feel like you are being ignored by the Holy One? You must boldly approach His throne of grace, and believe when you come to Him that He will meet your needs and answer your prayers. It is all available; just don't take no for an answer.

God doesn't want us to take no for an answer just for ourselves. It is also so we can help and be a blessing to others. Like the woman with the issue of blood, we as the body of Christ can have power coming from us to touch the lives of others. The Lord wants us to have such a powerful life with Him that whoever comes in contact with us will be forever changed by His power. It is especially important to not leave God alone so we can be a point of contact for someone else to be blessed by Him. Let me give you a couple of examples: one from the Scriptures, and the second from my life.

THE SYROPHOENICIAN WOMAN

In Matthew 15:22–28, this woman came to Jesus on behalf of someone else—her daughter who needed to be delivered. Have you ever gone to God on behalf of someone you knew? She approached Jesus so He would help her, and He responded with an example that sounded insulting. He used an illustration of a dog. In verse 26, Jesus said, "It is not right to take the children's bread and toss it to their dogs" (NIV). Doesn't that sound like an insult?

Being a Syrophoenician, she was not considered one of the children of the kingdom, and the "bread" she was asking for belonged to them. It sounded as if Jesus was calling her a dog not worthy of the answer she wanted. This woman, however, did not allow that to stop her. She continued to press and persist on the behalf of someone else even when it seemed she wouldn't get an answer. Once again it appeared Jesus didn't want to be bothered, and He told her He had been sent to the lost sheep of the house of Israel—and this didn't include her! This woman was desperate and determined not to leave without getting what she came for. She was stubborn in her heart at all costs. It may seem that a mighty God is ignoring you, but your determination is not going to change.

When Jesus saw this attitude in her, He took notice. He answered by saying, "Woman, you have great faith! Your request is granted" (verse 28, NIV). If you are ever concerned whether you have enough faith in your life, you can be confident that, if you won't take no for an answer, you will be like this woman. You have great faith!

THE NEIGHBOR WHO FELL FROM A BRIDGE

Another example of being persistent on behalf of someone else came at a time in my own life. I had a neighbor years ago who was still living in the hippie era. He dressed, talked, and acted like those who still lived in the sixties. In the natural he and I didn't have much in common. I had tried on many occasions to try to relate to him, but I didn't seem to get anywhere.

Then a few weeks before a tragic event in his life, the Lord spoke to my heart to pray for him more than I had ever done before. I did as God said to me and became persistent to pray for him. I believe the event that would follow turned out the way it did as a direct result of my prayers. I believe it saved his life. I still see in my mind the day his wife pulled into their driveway and began to help him out of their vehicle. He looked like a complete mummy with even his head wrapped in bandages. His eyes and mouth were about the only things visible.

A little while later, I finally found out what happened to him. He was a construction worker and had been working on a highway overpass bridge. He said he was prying back on a board, lost his balance, and started to fall. This hippie neighbor of mine said that all he could remember when he started to fall off the bridge was that he took a quick look at his co-worker, who was also on the bridge, and said, "Later!" Then he plummeted straight down. He told me that he landed in the mud below, with his rear end in the air, but unable to move. It was a miracle that he was still alive. He said the doctors were only concerned about brain damage, but they said he was lucky to be alive.

I know it wasn't luck but the result of persistent prayers of importunity calling out for the soul of this man. I was determined to have an opportunity to share the gospel with him, and this event gave it to me. I shared the gospel and some members of his family got saved, and he began to ask me questions about the Lord. It was those prayers that I prayed for someone else that kept this man alive and gave me an opportunity to witness to his family about Jesus. You can have the same opportunity. Someone needs you to be persistent and determined not to leave God alone on their behalf.

PRAYING AND NOT FAINTING

Jesus taught us in Luke 18:1 that we should pray without fainting. In other words, if we are praying, we won't be tempted to faint. It tells us that if we leave God alone we will become weak in our spiritual walk.

Just how do we know if we are becoming weak in prayer and our life is in danger of leaving God alone?

1. Are you leaving God alone? Is your prayer time inconsistent or nonexistent? Is it based only on when something is not going right for you? A key to overcoming a life of inconsistent prayer is to be determined to change. It is helpful if you establish a meeting time with Him. Treat your time with God as if you were meeting someone important. After all, He is important, isn't He? We would never think of not holding true to our commitment with someone we esteemed as famous. It is also important to choose a place to meet with Him. The key is to be persistent and consistent to do it.

2. Are you distracted in prayer? It is so easy to become distracted and discouraged when you truly decide to not leave God alone. You find yourself looking at the clock and your mind wandering away from focusing on prayer. We have all been there! Jesus gave us a helpful thing in Matthew 6:6. He told us to go into our prayer closet, shut the door, and pray in secret. He was encouraging us to find a place where we won't become distracted easily. It might be helpful before your time with God to make a list of what you want to pray about, and also make a list of things you have to do or things on your mind. This will help you clear your head and stay focused on what you want to talk to Him about. You might also consider praying in the spirit more. This will build your inner man so you won't become as distracted in the natural. If you are fainting in your pursuit of God, there will be certain signs.

3. Do you fall asleep in prayer? This is usually a sign you are growing weak in prayer. Sometimes true pursuit of Him can come at any hour or when you are exhausted from a hard day's work—the last thing you want to do is pray when you are tired. Sometimes it requires you to make yourself get up and "press" to pray. You might want to consider pacing, kneeling, walking, or sitting to help you stay awake while praying. Push yourself to stay focused and awake. It might be helpful to find someone who would agree to pray with you to help build a spiritual routine and accountability. Also try new things, and make prayer fun.

4. Do you only attempt to pray when things go wrong? This is what is often called crisis praying. It is praying only when things aren't going well. Remember, the more you refuse to leave God alone, even in the good times, the better your life will become. The best time to learn to become strong in your faith or learn to pray is not in the middle of the storm. It is much wiser to build your Christian foundation on His Word, prayer, and worship when things are going well so you are prepared for anything that might come in the future.

5. Does prayer feel boring? Every hungry person determined not to leave God alone has felt that they were just going through the motions at some point. You can't base your prayer life on how you feel. To help keep your prayer life from becoming stagnant, try putting on a worship tape that draws you into the spirit. Keep your prayer life creative and fun, and make God real to you. Make a list

of prayer requests so that you can chart answered prayer and encourage yourself.

6. Is your prayer time only at church or before a meal? A sign of a weak prayer life is when most of your praying is at church or before meals. Avoid that temptation by trying some new things in your prayer life. You might want to sing aloud, dance, lift your arms, or pray loudly. Simple things like that can make you want to pray more often.

7. Do you struggle to pray for any length of time? The true characteristic of those who don't leave God alone is they can't get enough of His time. Developing a strong prayer life needs to start small and build up. You can't try tomorrow to pray for hours when today you only prayed for minutes. Build up each week to where your prayer time grows. Jesus pressed and grew His prayer. When He seemed finished with prayer, He went on a little more. Mark 14:35 says, "Going a little farther, he fell to the ground and prayed..." (NIV). Set a time and build up from there. You might want to do what I did during the time when the Lord said to me, "Please don't leave," and not restrict yourself to a certain amount of time. This will help us do what Jesus wanted His disciples to do. Jesus said, "Could you not watch one hour?" (Mark 11:37, NKJV). Eventually you will get to where one hour doesn't seem like much.

Jesus is waiting for your response today. What will you say to Him? God does not want to be left alone. It is not good for you to leave Him alone. He is waiting for you to press into Him. Just as He called to Adam in the garden by saying, "Where are you?" He doesn't want to be alone and is looking for you to meet with Him. He wants to walk and talk with you. Your success in life comes from including God and having His involvement in all you do and in every part of your life.

Your freedom and blessing are found when you *don't leave God alone*!

Perhaps after reading this book you realize you have never known Jesus Christ in a personal way, and you want an intimate relationship with Him. I want to encourage you to begin a new life right now of knowing Him and not leaving Him alone.

My prayer is that you will spend quality time with Him every day. Go ahead and ask Him to fill your heart with His presence and to draw you deeper into a more meaningful relationship with Him. Your new life of not leaving God alone begins now!

I want to personally invite you to pray this prayer and receive the promise of eternal life with Him forever!

> *Dear heavenly Father, I dedicate my life from this moment forward to not leaving You alone. I will pursue You like those I have read about, and I ask You to bless me and my life in the ways You blessed them. In my heart, I truly believe that Your Son, Jesus Christ, died on the cross for me and rose from the dead so I can live forever with You in heaven. You said whoever would call on the name of Jesus would be saved from their sins. I ask You, Jesus, to come into my heart and life. I ask You to forgive me for all my sins, I repent of my wrongdoings, and I commit to live a life that pleases You. Fill me with Your Holy Spirit and draw me closer to You! From this moment forward, I say I am a Christian, a true lover and follower of Jesus Christ. I desire to know You more than ever before, and today I choose to not leave You alone until You bless me!*

Remember friend: DLGA! Don't Leave God Alone! He is waiting for you.

ONE VOICE MINISTRIES

THE MINISTRY OF
HANK & BRENDA KUNNEMAN

CONFERENCES

Hank and Brenda travel worldwide, ministering in churches, conferences, and conventions. They bring relevant biblical messages from a prophetic viewpoint, and their dynamic preaching style is coupled with demonstrations of the Holy Spirit. Though they preach at events separately, they are especially known for their unique platform of ministry together as a team in the ministry of the gifts of the Spirit. For additional information about scheduling a ministry or church conference with either or both of them, contact One Voice Ministries at (402) 896-6692 or request a ministry packet online at www.ovm.org.

BOOKS, PRODUCTS, AND RESOURCES

Books, audio, and video material are available at the ministry online store at www.ovm.org. Book titles include When Your Life Has Been Tampered With, Hide and Seek, and Chaos in the King's Court. The One Voice Ministries' Web site also provides many ministry resources, including Hank's page called "Prophetic Perspectives" that includes excerpts and prophetic insight on world events. Brenda's page, "The Daily Prophecy," has changed lives around the world. There are also numerous articles for study.

LORD OF HOSTS CHURCH

Hank and Brenda Kunneman also pastor Lord of Hosts Church in Omaha, Nebraska. Filled with captivating praise and worship and sound, prophetic teaching, services at Lord of Hosts Church are always rich with the presence of God. Lord of Hosts Church is known for its solid team of leaders, organized style, and ministry that touches the everyday needs of people. Through the many avenues of ministry the church is raising up strong believers. Many ministries worldwide have referred to Lord of Hosts Church as being one of the most up and coming, cutting-edge churches in the United States. For further information about Lord of Hosts Church, call (402) 896-6692, or visit online at www.lohchurch.org or www.ovm.org.

PASTORS HANK AND BRENDA KUNNEMAN
LORD OF HOSTS CHURCH AND ONE VOICE MINISTRIES

5351 S. 139th PLAZA • OMAHA, NE 68137
PHONE (402) 896-6692 • FAX (402) 894-9068
WWW.OVM.ORG • WWW.LOHCHURCH.ORG

Strang Communications, publisher of both **Charisma House** and *Charisma* magazine, wants to give you

3 FREE ISSUES

of our **award-winning** magazine.

www.charismamag.com

Since its inception in 1975, *Charisma* magazine has helped thousands of Christians stay connected with what God is doing worldwide.

Within its pages you will discover in-depth reports and the latest news from a Christian perspective, biblical health tips, global events in the body of Christ, personality profiles, and so much more. Join the family of *Charisma* readers who enjoy feeding their spirit each month with miracle-filled testimonies and inspiring articles that bring clarity, provoke prayer, and demand answers.

To claim your **3 free issues** of *Charisma*, send your name and address to: Charisma 3 Free Issue Offer, 600 Rinehart Road, Lake Mary, FL 32746. Or you may call **1-800-829-3346** and ask for Offer #**97FREE**. This offer is only valid in the USA.

Charisma
+CHRISTIAN LIFE
www.charismamag.com

7347